Profitable New Scrapbooking Business

Profitable New Scrapbooking Business

Lee Lister is a Business Consultant with more than 25 year's consultancy experience for many household names. She is known as The Bid Manager or The Biz Guru.

From an early age they began an unparalleled journey through business consulting that continues to span across the UK, USA, Europe and Asia. She has consulted for many companies all over the world. Specialising in business change management, start up consultancy and trouble shooting. She is highly skilled in seminars, lectures and corporate presentations on business, project management and bid management. Lee's experience in marketing and internet marketing is also keenly sought after.

She is a prolific publisher and writer of books, ebooks and articles on business, entrepreneurship and bid management. They can easily be found on major search engines and Amazon.

Profitable New Scrapbooking Business

Profitable New Scrapbooking Business

Learn how to set up a profitable business, understand how to overcome the strains and stresses of a new company and become a Successful Entrepreneur.

www.ProfitableNewBusiness.com

Author: Lee Lister

No part of this publication may be reproduced, stored in a retrieval system, or transmitted in any form or by any means, without the prior permission in writing of the publisher nor be otherwise circulated in any form of binding or cover other than that in which it is published and without a similar condition including this condition being imposed on the subsequent purchaser. This book may not be used as a training course in any format.

© Copyright Lee Lister 2011
All rights reserved.
Published by: Biz Guru Ltd
Photo Copyright: © Kudryashka

ISBN: 978-1-907551-05-5

This book is dedicated to my daughter Kerry Lister for whom I have always strived to be my best.

Other books available include:
Entrepreneur's Apprentice
How Much Does It Cost To Start A Business?
Profitable New Party Selling Business
Profitable New Cake Decorating Business
Profitable New Manicurist Business
Profitable New Quilting Business
Profitable New Bottled Water Business

Profitable New Scrapbooking Business

Contents

Legal Notice -- **11**

Introduction -- **12**

What Kind Of Scrapbooking Business? ----------------- **15**

Scrapbooking Sales Consultant ------------------------ **16**

Scrapbooking Instructor --------------------------------- **19**

Scrapbooking Event Organiser ------------------------- **25**

Product Designer --------------------------------------- **28**

Scrapbooking Expert ------------------------------------ **30**

Scrapbook Artist -- **34**

Scrapbook Retailer ------------------------------------- **37**

EBay And Paper Piecing --------------------------------- **39**

    Creating Piecings That Will Sell----------------------------42

    Organization---43

    Advertising Your Auction----------------------------------43

    Custom Orders --44

    Provide Excellent Customer Service-----------------------46

Target Audience -- **47**

Your Business Kit -------------------------------------- **49**

    Your Brochure---49

    Business Cards--50

    Uniform--50

    Your Sales Pack---50

Your Equipment -- **52**

    Tools---52

    Albums---54

    Paper--55

    Embellishments--56

    Storage--56

    Office Kit--58

Profitable New Scrapbooking Business

Storage And Inventory Control — 59
Pricing Your Services — 61
A Successful Business Start up — 62
Your Business Framework — 65
The Nasties — 67
Check List For Starting A New Business — 68
How Much Does It Cost To Start A Business? — 71
    Check List – Business Start Up Costs — 74
Will I Succeed? — 75
Getting Started With Little Money — 77
What Goes Into A Business Plan? — 79
Meeting The Bank Manager — 82
Some Scrapbooking Themes — 84
    Coming of a Baby — 85
    Wedding and Wedding Anniversaries — 86
    Graduation — 87
    Title — 88
    Colour — 89
Scrapbooking Tips — 90
    Photographs — 90
    Cutting and Cropping — 91
    Order — 92
    Text — 92
    Tags — 93
    Embellishments — 93
    Patterning — 94
    Spacing — 95
    Mounting — 96
    Getting Rid of Messes and Mistakes — 96
    Preservation — 97

Newspaper Clippings --- 97
Graphics and Clipart --- 98
Weaving Photographs --- 98
Collage --- 99
Photograph Mosaics --- 100
Markers --- 100
Wax Pencils --- 101
Stickers --- 101
Rubber Stamping --- 102
Faux Wax Seals --- 103
Tearing --- 103
Fraying --- 103
Curled Edges --- 104
Antique Look --- 104
Leather Look --- 104
Accents --- 105
Punching --- 105
Coloured Paper --- 106
Vellum --- 106
Shadow Boxes --- 107
Adding Dimension --- 107
Common Business Mistakes. --- 108
Standing Out From The Crowd --- 111
So how do I define my USP? --- 111
Branding, The How's, What's And Why's --- 112
What is Branding? --- 112
I Do not Have that Kind of Money - So Why do I Need to Create my Own Brand? --- 113
So How Do I Create My Own Brand Then? --- 114
What Should Be Described Within My Brand? --- 115

Profitable New Scrapbooking Business

    Tag Line — 115

    Logo's — 116

Working with your Brand — 117

    Branding, Packaging and other Stuff — 117

    Business Name — 117

    Packaging — 118

    Marketing Material — 118

Starting Small With Your Premises — 119

    Mall Karts and Kiosks — 119

    Marketing From Your Retail Site — 121

Marketing Your Business — 122

    Other Marketing Tools — 124

Tips to Overcoming Stage Fright — 126

Giving A Compelling Presentation — 128

    10 Tips for Professional Speakers — 129

Seminars — 132

    Setting Up Your Seminar — 132

    Organising Your Seminar — 134

    Charisma Matters! — 136

    Tips to Overcoming Stage Fright — 138

    Back of the Room Sales? — 140

Party Selling — 144

    Administration — 145

    Your First Party — 146

    Recruiting New Hosts — 149

    Advertising — 150

    Secrets of Success — 151

Trade Shows And Conventions — 153

Interacting With Your Customers — 155

    Scrapbooking Consultancy Services — 155

Profitable New Scrapbooking Business

    Estimating -- 156

    Seminars, Workshops and Training Courses ------------- 158

The Art of Selling -- 159

Administration --- 161

    Customer Administration ------------------------------- 162

Writing A Winning Proposal? -------------------------- 163

Putting Your Business On The Internet -------------- 165

    As A Shop Window ------------------------------------- 165

    As A Full Site --- 166

    Factors To Remember --------------------------------- 166

An Internet Marketing Strategy ----------------------- 167

Staff --- 171

Customer Contracts --- 172

    Why Do I Need Contracts? ----------------------------- 172

    Written and Verbal Contracts -------------------------- 173

    Will It Be Expensive? ----------------------------------- 173

    Contracts for Small Purchases. ------------------------ 174

The Top 5 First Year Mistakes --------------------------- 175

    Waiting for Customers to Come to You ---------------- 175

    Spending Too Much on Advertising -------------------- 175

    Being Too Nice -- 176

    Not Using the Phone ---------------------------------- 177

    Hiring Professionals for Everything -------------------- 177

Problems You May Have ---------------------------------- 178

Time for a Holiday: But How? ------------------------- 179

    Tell People When You Are Going Away. ---------------- 179

    Change Your Voicemail Message. --------------------- 180

    Set Up an Email Auto responder. ---------------------- 180

    Do not Stay Away Too Long. -------------------------- 181

    Get Someone to Look after the Business. -------------- 181

Profitable New Scrapbooking Business

In Conclusion -- 182
Index: -- 183

Legal Notice

We do not believe in get rich quick schemes. We do believe that business is equal parts of inspiration, hard work and luck. We ensure that every book that we sell will be interesting and useful to our clients. Every effort has been made to accurately represent our product and it is potential.

Please remember that each individual's success depends on their background, dedication, desire, and motivation. As with any business endeavour, there is **no guarantee that you will earn any money**. This book will provide you with a number of suggestions you can use to better guarantee your chances for success. **We do not and cannot guarantee any level of profits.**

Any and every business venture contains risks and any number of alternatives. We do not suggest that any one way is the right way or that our suggestions are the only way. On the contrary, we advise that before investing any money in a business venture you seek advice from a qualified accountant and/or attorney.

You read and use this book on the strict understanding that you alone are responsible for the success or failure of your business decisions relating to any information presented by our company Biz Guru Ltd.

Profitable New Scrapbooking Business

Introduction

Scrapbooking has been around for years. Teenagers have taped prom tickets to notebook pages and written their memories of the evening along with pictures and other mementos. Families arrange photos into albums and perhaps label them with dates and other information. Travellers make notes of places visited, perhaps saving tickets, postcards or other mementos.

Scrapbooking as we now know it got its official start in 1980 by the Christensen family in Utah, USA. These pioneers went on to launch the hugely successful company Keeping Memories Alive. It is been almost 30 years, but the scrapbook industry continues to grow at an exponential rate.

In the last several years, scrapbooking has taken on a new life. No longer are these albums simply photos and labels or a couple of prom tickets taped to a page. Now they are elaborately styled memory books with fancy embellishments and features. Some people consider scrapbooking an art form, and when you look at some of these pages, you might just agree.

Scrapbooking has blossomed into a billion dollar business. In fact, the latest figures reveal that it is now a $2.55 billion per year business - and that is only in the U.S.! If true figures were to be told, the amount would certainly be well over $5 billion.

Profitable New Scrapbooking Business

The concept behind scrapbooking hasn't changed much. You still place photographs, newspaper clippings, poems, and tickets into a scrapbook to display and preserve your memories. However, scrapbooking techniques and tools have matured substantially in the last few years. Scrapbooking albums have replaced the messy bundles of paper. Albums are generally bound or placed in a three-ring binder so that your hard work will not fall apart.

Paste is also a thing of the past. Specialised glue dots and two-sided tape makes mounting treasures simple and mess free. Many of these products are so strong that you can now decorate scrapbook pages with ribbons, feathers, flowers, or even metal charms.

Due to these new techniques and tools, the uses of scrapbooking have expanded drastically. Scrapbooking is still used to hold personal keepsakes and for gift giving. However, now scrapbooking techniques can be used to make baby announcements, grandparent books, gift cards, artwork for kid's rooms, recipe books, and even educational tools.

Many people are cashing in on the craze by starting their own scrapbooking businesses. There are many, many ways to make money if you love to scrapbook. Perhaps the biggest advantage of starting your own scrapbooking business is that it can be done for a relatively small start-up investment.

Profitable New Scrapbooking Business

What we have done with this book is compile tips and tricks from people who've successfully started their own scrapbooking business. You will learn so much in these pages: how to name your business, what supplies you will need, what to charge for your services, marketing your business, and finding creative ways to get your name out there.

You can pursue this business in many different ways. You can create pages for other people, you can sell scrapping supplies, or you can become a consultant for others teaching them how to do their own scrapbooks. Whichever route you choose, scrapbooking can be profitable and fun!

Many people think the only way to build a business in the scrapbooking world is by opening a retail store - not true! There are more than a dozen other ways you can make a living in this industry and some of them are much more profitable than retail!

What Kind Of Scrapbooking Business?

There are many different ways that you can start your own scrapbooking business:

- Sales consultant.
- Scrapbooking instructor.
- Event organiser.
- Product Designer.
- Scrapbooking Expert.
- Scrapbooking Artist.
- Scrapbooking Retailer.

Each one of the types of business has their own merits and their own problems. Being a scrapbooking retailer has the largest start up costs, although you can mitigate these by starting with a kart in the mall or a market stall. The scrapbooking expert is probably the hardest to do, but you build up to this by building your brand and marketing your business, you will also need more writing sills with this option. The other business options really need you to have a lot of stock and some good planning skills. Whichever business option you try, and you can have more than one type of business if you wish, this book seeks to advise you of the best way forward. Let us start by reviewing the different ways that you can have a business, utilising your love of scrapbooking.

Scrapbooking Sales Consultant

This is the way most people break into the industry and the most common method is by party selling. We have a whole book dedicated to party selling – Profitable New Party Selling which details how to run this kind of business.

If you do want to work as a consultant to another company, we strongly suggest doing your homework first. What are you looking for when choosing a company to go with?

First, look at the products they have available. Successful sales consultants exude a genuine enthusiasm for their products so you need to understand and love your products. It is important for you to get your hands on the products before you make any legal commitments. Place an order or, at the very least, request a catalogue and samples before joining any company.

Start up cost also has to be a factor. What kind of cash outlay will your start-up require? Look closely at the company's joining fee and/or the cost of your business starter kit, but also think realistically about how much inventory you will need to have on hand.

What kinds of business supplies or products you will need to get your business started? You might also look at how the products are usually sold. If you want to sell on auction sites lie eBay their may be restrictions.

Profitable New Scrapbooking Business

If you do not want to sell via party selling a company that concentrates on this type of selling is obviously not for you.

Does the company you are considering going with require any monthly minimums? If they do, you need to think long and hard about whether or not you are ready to invest the time and effort into making your quotas. Of course, the harder you work, the more money you make. Be passionate about the company and what they have to offer. You must convince yourself they are the best before you can convince others.

Look at the commission rate the company is offering. Each direct sales plan is different, and it is important to look over the fine print. What is the commission rate and how is it paid? How are you awarded for recruiting others? How does the company handle breakaways?

Are you sure that this is not some kind of illegal pyramid system? If the concentration is on finding people to join the company and pay start up fees rather than helping your build sales of your products, you are probably looking at a pyramid scheme!

Before you sign on, find out how much control you will have over marketing the products. Most companies have a "rule book" you can reference. You will want to have enough lee-way to successfully promote your business and the products you have for sale.

Profitable New Scrapbooking Business

See if the company has any type of support system in place. You are bound to have questions arise from time to time. A reputable company will offer you the expertise and know-how of their staff to help you along.

Does the company offer any type of advertising for you to use? Marketing and advertising are crucial to business success. The bigger the audience, the more success you will have. If your company does some type of national advertising, this can only benefit you even more.

You should also find out their requirements for using their company name and logo. The last thing you want to do is advertise the company you are selling for in the wrong way.

What is unique about the company? Do they have any products that are distributed exclusively by them? This can make you stand out from your competition. Also, take a look at the level of saturation in your particular market. A newer company that offers quality products may hold a lot of promise in your particular industry.

Finally, if the company has an e-commerce option, it should have a huge advantage over the others. Many direct sales companies are now offering replicated websites so each representative can promote an individual online presence. A few direct sales companies even have shopping carts alongside these websites so you can make sales online, too, with the product drop shipped from your home office.

Scrapbooking Instructor

If you think that you have a flair for teaching, teaching scrapbooking in classes and workshops at your local scrapbook store or on your own can be a good way to bring in some extra money. While this might seem like an easy way to run a business there are actually a lot of things to take into consideration before you venture into teaching.

Obviously, you are going to have to be nearly an expert in the field before you can show other people how to scrapbook, but that just takes practice. This is a good way to promote direct sales as well if you have decided to sell scrapbooking products.

There are literally hundreds of people out there – even in the smallest town – who want to learn how to preserve their memories in gorgeous, impressive scrapbooks. The key here is marketing yourself and your classes in the most cost-efficient way possible.

The great thing about scrapbooking is that almost everyone has pictures. Anyone can learn to scrapbook. A passion to teach others how to preserve their family memories is a great quality to have if considering being a scrapbook instructor.

If you have a local scrapbook store, contact them and see if you might be able to hold a class at their facility.

Profitable New Scrapbooking Business

Usually, they are happy to accommodate since they are selling the supplies that you will be using, so their sales are almost guaranteed to rise during your workshop.

Contact store owners and talk to them about being a "guest teacher" or a regular instructor at their store. Make an appointment with the store owner so that you can bring samples of projects and layouts that you have done. Have a list handy of all of the classes that you have taught or classes that you are willing to teach.

If you do not have a scrapbook store or want to hold the workshop on your own, look into renting out a facility. You may also be able to find free accommodations with a local community centre or senior citizen facility. This is a great hobby for the senior set, so you may want to trade services for facilities to instruct the older community.

When picking out a place to hold your class, make sure it is well-lit and that there is plenty of room for everyone to spread out and work efficiently.

When having classes, pick out a theme. A good rule of thumb is to schedule classes about 2 weeks after an important event. Then centre your instruction on creating pages from the photos that your students have taken. Some ideas for occasions should include:
- Christmas
- Easter
- Valentine's Day

- Fourth of July
- Graduation
- New Year's
- First Day of School
- Thanksgiving
- Summer Vacation or Holidays

You'll also want to schedule periodic classes for other special occasions such as:
- Weddings
- Engagements
- Sports
- Military
- Retirement
- Anniversary
- Pregnancies
- Baby shower or similar

You need to figure out what your costs are going to be and how much you will need to make to realise a profit. Most instructors will charge a registration fee. You shouldn't make it too steep or people will be discouraged. You need to decide if you will be supplying materials and include these costs, or if the people attending will have to purchase the supplies themselves or bring along their own. Always have some supplies to hand for those that misunderstand or forget!

Profitable New Scrapbooking Business

Keep in mind that you will be teaching people how to put together their own scrapbooks. This will be much easier if you are teaching everyone with the same materials. Consider raising the entry fee a little and providing all entrants with the materials they will need to create a memorable scrapbook page.

Make sure your students understand from the outset what will be included in the class and what they need to provide, along with the time, date and cost. It might be a good idea to place these details on your advert and receipts.

Email or call your students beforehand as you will make loyal learners by your cheery call. Tell them you are glad they are coming to your class and remind them of cost, supplies they will need to bring and any added benefits...such as "Remember, you'll get 10 percent off anything you purchase the night of the workshop, so bring your wish list!"

Ask if they have any questions ahead of time and add a request that they provide 24 hours notice if something comes up. Consider having a 24-hour cancellation policy unless there is an emergency.

When making up your class ideas, make some notes on any tricky things involved. What may seem simple to you might cause problems for new scrapbookers.

Profitable New Scrapbooking Business

Look your sample over with a critical eye and see if there is anything that takes extra explanation or time, or if there is a new product that everyone might not have used.

You may also want to provide a free gift for attendees. One instructor reports that they likes to order bulk quantities of stickers and papers and hand them out at her classes to give her students the added satisfaction of getting something just for showing up.

Even better, add your logo and company name so they remember you. We all love free stuff, do not we? Your students will too!

When teaching the class, there are a few things you need to keep in mind to be successful.

First and foremost, be prepared. Review your class materials the night before so they are fresh in your mind. Have a checklist of everything that you need to take along to a class. Show up early and have the room set up before people arrive. Be enthusiastic. Even if you are feeling sluggish or having a bad day, you need to always be enthusiastic and smiling during your classes.

Be personable. Try to make eye contact and/or talk to each and every person in your class. Keep an eye out for anyone that may need extra attention and be willing to offer help to them if needed.

Profitable New Scrapbooking Business

Always thank everyone for coming to class. Have evaluations forms that can be filled out and use them to improve any future classes.

Take some of your profit and send out Thank You cards to all the students who attended your event. Since you'll probably be hosting other classes, they will remember your personal touch and are more likely to come back for more classes or better still, bring some friends with them.

Scrapbooking Event Organiser

There are retreats, crops, getaways, cruises, conventions, and more being held every single weekend now! Scrapbookers love to connect, and you can help provide the connection. If you are well-organised and can put together the kind of event that will generate excellent word-of-mouth, an event planning company could be a profitable venture for you.

While this is along the same lines as teaching a class, events are meant to be all day affairs – even multiple day affairs. So many women are hankering to get out of the house and get away from the stresses of every day life. A weekend scrapbooking retreat would be right up their alley!

One website we have found gives an account of her "Scrap Camp" that they hosts where a camping experience combines with scrapbooking to provide attendees with not only a getaway, but a way to talk and interact with other scrapbookers and get ideas from each other.

Just like the classes, you'll need to set a price and decide whether or not supplies are included in the price. Obviously, the cost is going to be a bit higher, but often times, your attendees will not blink an eye to paying it.

Profitable New Scrapbooking Business

Concentrate a multiple day event on putting together an entire scrapbook. Encourage your students to bring along as many pictures as they can find and then show them how to organise them into beautiful layouts.

An event might require you to spend more one-on-one time with those attending, but personal service could be the difference between you and your competition.

Contact scrapbooking suppliers and let them know about your event. See if they would be willing to donate supplies in exchange for liberal advertising at your event. You might be surprised at how many companies would be happy to sponsor T-shirts, flyers, and even supplies. This is especially true if you really play up your event and have great attendance.

If you can find a company willing to donate toward your event, you want to keep them on your valuable contacts list. The best way to do this is to send a follow-up after the event is over to show how successful your event and their products were.

You can do this in many ways. We would suggest having all participants sign an over-sized card with personal comments and include pictures of that company's products being used. They will surely appreciate the advertising and are more likely to sponsor one of your other events further down the road.

Profitable New Scrapbooking Business

The best part about scrapbooking events is that you can plan other activities to go along with classes to enhance the experience. After all, you really do not want to spend 12 hours doing nothing but scrapbooking, do you? It would seem too much like work.

Even though scrapbooking is the main reason for the event, networking, sharing ideas, and making friends is also important. This is an excellent way to promote scrapbooking in your community and share your love of the hobby.

Product Designer

Many scrapbooking products were designed by scrapbook enthusiasts, who saw the need for a product and filled it. Product designers can either license their idea to a larger manufacturer or take the plunge and start their own company!

Success stories abound in this industry about people who went from an idea to a multi-product corporation. Of course, going it alone also means an investment of time and money, so be sure you have both before starting your company.

What types of qualities does a product designer need? Above all, creativity is the best thing you can offer. Perhaps you have come up with an excellent new die cut.

How about inventing a new pair of decorative scissors? When you are a product designer, literally anything is possible.

You need to find a niche that hasn't been filled. Then do product research. See if your idea is feasible and what kind of investment you'll need to make in order to bring it to reality.

Profitable New Scrapbooking Business

Use the library or Internet to locate information about your product. While conducting your research, you'll notice that products with a good reputation or success story are easily located. That is because companies who've had success with a product are not afraid to boast about it.

Rely on your experience. All great success stories begin with a person that has knowledge or a great interest in the product they are selling. Is the product interesting to you? Will you use it on a continuing basis? What is the life expectancy of the product? Do you know people that are familiar with the product?

Contact a scrapbook supplier and tell them about your idea. See if they think it has marketable potential. A word of caution here – do not be too specific about your new idea. You do not want to risk someone "honing in" on your new invention.

However, an informed opinion about the product's potential in the marketplace and value is possible after you have gathered all the information possible. All you really need to know now is if there is a real need for this product in the marketplace so do not rush into making a decision prior to bringing all of your tools to bear analyzing the item.

Scrapbooking Expert

Scrapbook enthusiasts who get published in the major magazines and idea books sometimes develop a "fan club" of other scrapbookers. That fame can sometimes be translated into connections with manufacturers to teach nationally or design products, retailers as "celebrity" guests, and other industry opportunities. So go ahead, submit your pages!

This is akin to being a freelance writer. If you think you have created an especially beautiful page, send a picture to a scrapbooking magazine. If they publish it, you have made it! If they do not, keep trying.

Start out by subscribing to at least four of the major scrapbooking magazines. Some to consider would be:
- Creating Keepsakes
- Memory Makers
- Simple Scrapbooks
- Paper Kuts
- Paper Crafts
- Your Creative Spirit

When submitting your pages, you have two options. You can scan your layout and submit it through e-mail or you can make a colour copy and send it through "snail mail". If you make copies to send, your costs can add up, especially if you are submitting to multiple magazines. Email might be your best option,

Profitable New Scrapbooking Business

With each layout submission, you'll need to include your name, address, phone number, email, and supply list. The supply list is important, as magazines will not publish your layout without one. If you are working on a layout you think you'll want to submit, keep track of what supplies you use and the manufacturer of each one. Be as detailed as you can!

You can submit the same layout to every magazine, but be aware that when one magazine publishes your layout, other magazines will not use the same one. If you decide to submit, it is also a good idea to take those layouts off of the popular Web sites.

Magazines typically keep layouts on file and will ask for them when the need arises for a layout like yours. You might be contacted months down the line, so try and be patient. Sometimes the magazines will say what types of layouts they are looking for in advance. Check the magazines and their Web sites.

Remember that most magazines are working on issues that will not be out for months, so your Christmas page may be being considered in the summer.

Just do it! I've heard from so many scrapbookers that they have not been published, but they "have not submitted as much as they should." Write it on your To-Do list! Schedule a time to submit your layouts on a regular basis.

Profitable New Scrapbooking Business

It may seem elusive, but consider that the magazines need to fill space with as many excellent layouts as they can. So keep submitting!

If you are going to be published, the excitement will be great the day you get the call! Be ready for some down time while you wait for the issue to come out, and then it is excitement time again! You'll usually get your layout back when the next issue of the magazine is published.

If more than one magazine chooses to publish a layout, you'll need to tell the other magazines that unfortunately, another magazine contacted you first.

Some magazines pay with product and others with cash. But the opportunity to put "published designer" after your name is priceless! Good luck!

Set up your own website and publish your amazing pages on there. Offer up complete instructions on how people can re-create those pages for a small fee.

Once you have established a "name" by being published, you can approach manufacturers (or they might approach you first!) about teaching for them at national conventions and trade shows. That "name" might also unlock the door to getting your own product ideas and designs licensed to a large manufacturer.

Profitable New Scrapbooking Business

Retailers can advertise the fact that they, or staff members and instructors, are "published designers." There is much power behind those words! Scrapbookers want to learn from the best, and some aspire (even in their own minds) to be the best – and what better way than to hang out with the "stars" and hope some of it rubs off!

Scrapbook Artist

There is a growing market for those who make scrapbooks for others. The appeal for scrapbook enthusiasts is great – minimal start-up costs - you really can start with almost nothing! You get to work from home; choose your hours, and how much you want to charge.

See, a lot of people like the look of scrapbooks, but do not have the time, knowledge, or creativity to do it themselves. And, as with other service businesses such as professional organizing and interior design, it is easier for some people to hire out than to do it themselves.

This business has really started to grow and hard-working professional scrapbook artists who believe in their service and promote it to the target markets who understand what it is worth can grow their businesses very quickly. This service has the potential for the most income – but again, that success is ultimately up to you.

Professional scrapbook artists who make scrapbooks for others can certainly use the fact that they have been published as a draw. Include it in your marketing materials, on your Web site, in your portfolio, etc.

Profitable New Scrapbooking Business

As a scrapbook business owner, you have clients supply you with their photos and you use creativity and you artistic ideas to design the books. Professional scrap bookers also offer the written word and catchy captions to increase their marketability.

Anyone can throw some pictures, letters, postcards, and the like into a scrapbook. People who want the services of a scrapbooking business, however, are looking for more. They want scrapbooks that are more than just things flung between the covers of a scrapbook to show their family members and friends.

Often people want to be sure they leave behind a legacy and hiring a professional to put together their life and memories is something many people will pay a lot of money for. Sometimes you will be asked to piece together fifty years of someone's life in a chronological order of presentation. This includes anything from articles, high school items, pictures, certificates, etc.

This is a great gift business. A professionally designed scrapbook makes a wonderful gift for someone's monumental birthday or special occasion, like retirement.

When you decide to make scrapbook pages for other people, a website can be crucial to your business success. With the worldwide web, you can attract customers globally instead of just locally. Of course, this will take a little know-how and a lot of customer service on your part.

Profitable New Scrapbooking Business

You can have your customers e-mail you their photos or they can mail them to you. You need to thoroughly interview them as to what they are expecting from the pages you create for them.

You are going to have to spend a lot of time talking with your clients to get the real story behind the photos, but it will be worth it for both you and them! When you are able to journal the events behind the pictures, the pages will be especially special. They are hiring you to preserve their memories – you do not want to let them down!

If you prefer, you can have them do their own journaling and then hire an outside service to turn that handwriting into its own font so you can print it out and include it in the scrapbook. Keep in mind this service will cost extra and it should be included in your bottom line cost to them.

You may want to devise some type of questionnaire that they can fill out online and submit it to you. Payment options are important as well. Consider signing up for Pay Pal if you have not already. You will be able to accept credit cards through this service without paying extra fees to each credit card company.

Scrapbook Retailer

A few years ago, opening a retail scrapbook store was a viable option for most people who wanted to get involved in the industry. Although it can still be a successful venture for many, certain circumstances need to be examined carefully before jumping in.

A large initial investment and time commitment are needed, as well as detailed research into your local area of present and potential competition. Profits differ, depending on the area demographics and competition, and though many stores report not taking home a pay check for at least the first year, other stores are quite profitable and open multiple locations.

This is the most expensive way to get into scrapbooking as a business. You will have to purchase a large amount of inventory and find a storefront to operate out of.

However, this can be a very profitable venture when you consider all of the options that you will have available to you. You can bring in guest instructors to teach classes for you which will increase your sales – especially if they use your inventory to create their pages.

Profitable New Scrapbooking Business

You can schedule weekly crop nights where fellow scrapbookers get together and put together their pages. Charge a small fee for this service and offer up your expertise as a professional to help them in making a memorable page. Making it a social night will be very attractive to groups of friends who want an excuse for a night out.

You could also consider opening a market stall or kiosk rather than a shop and we discuss these options further on in the book.

You might also consider selling your supplies via party planning. Setting up parties or nights out with a group of friends, partly teaching scrapbooking and partly selling your products. This is another way of negating the high costs of a retail store.

EBay And Paper Piecing

This is an amazingly lucrative way to make money by using your scrapbooking expertise and taking advantage of the global marketplace that is eBay!

What is paper piecing? Basically, you put together pre-made scrapbook pages and sell them to people online. All they have to do is add their pictures and any journaling they want to write down and their scrapbook page will be complete.

Initial research on eBay shows that people are willing to pay for this service which can be an amazing way for you to make a lot of money with scrapbooking!

If you are unfamiliar with selling on eBay, it is really quite easy to do. You'll first need to set up a selling account. It is a good idea to include "scrap" in your name if possible. Once you have your user name, you'll need to establish your selling account. This usually means providing a credit card or bank account to eBay and verifying it before you get started. Do not worry – it is safe and secure.

We could write a whole entire other book on getting started selling on eBay but that is not necessary just visit eBay's website and review their very good information.

Profitable New Scrapbooking Business

Review the kind of products that sell well on the site and when you have some product you want to sell, take pictures of it or scan it into your computer. Pictures will be a huge selling point, so make sure they are of good quality and you provide as many as you possibly can to give potential customers a better idea of what the product looks like. In your title, include the words "paper piecing" (without the quotation marks) since that's how people will search for listings.

List the dimensions and a brief description of each part of the set. Also let people know if you used pens and chalks to add detail to your sets. If any part of your set is computer generated, it is a good idea to note this in the auction. Let everyone know whether your background paper is included or not.

Make sure you let your potential customers know if you use all acid-free, lignin-free products when making your sets. A lot of people also list information such as "comes from a pet-free, smoke-free home."

At the end of the description list all payment and shipping information. You want to make sure that customers know the following: what payment methods you accept/prefer, your shipping rate, how the items will be packed, whether or not you offer insurance and how much you charge. You might find it useful to open a PayPal account as this seems to be the most popular payment method – primarily because eBay owns PayPal!

Profitable New Scrapbooking Business

Set the price at the absolute minimum you are willing to accept for this paper piecing. Most auctions start in the $3-10 range. Adjust your minimum bid price according to time, materials used, and the detail of the piece.

You have a choice of 3, 5, 7, and 10 day auctions. Most paper pieces use either 5 or 7 day auctions. It is a good idea to have your auction last over a Sunday evening because it is a very busy time.

Each time you create an original paper piecing it automatically has copyright protection. You do not need to register a creation to have it protected. It is a good idea to put a notice with your auctions when it is an original design. If you are using a pattern from a Tole/Pattern book, you should not use a copyright notice. A basic copyright notice looks like this: Copyright 2011: Name

This also means that all of those other original paper piecings that are listed on eBay are protected. It is okay to browse around and get ideas and inspiration, but you should never make copies of paper piecing that you see. Also you must not use other people's copyrighted images in your piecings – this includes such matters as Disney characters for example.

Profitable New Scrapbooking Business

Creating Piecings That Will Sell

Save some time by eliminating the "tracing" of patterns. Take your pattern, lay it over your cardstock and use your stylus to "trace" it onto your cardstock. You won't need a light box or copier for this and you can re-use your patterns again and again.

Use the Fiskars soft-tip micro-touch ones. They have an ultra fine tip that will allow you to get into small spaces and make precision cuts. You should also try to move your paper around instead of moving the scissors. This will allow you to cut a smooth and even line.

Sets that have more than one matching piece do better than a stand alone paper piecing. Even a title or matching smaller accent piece of paper helps! Other things that help are matching tags, journaling boxes, corners, borders, or stickers.

Learn how to do details. Invest in a very thin tipped black pen and a white gel pen to add detail to your pieces. Use lots of shading on your paper piecings. Shade with chalk - use the small pompoms with hemostats to hold the pompom to do your chalking and shading in small places.

Take a look at some tole books to learn how to create proper shading on your sets. Practice shading techniques by taking a household object and shining a light on it then noting where the shadows and highlights fall. Move the light and see how the shading changes.

Profitable New Scrapbooking Business

Make your paper piecings special or unique. Try to use the latest scrapbooking trends in new and unusual ways. Pay attention to colour schemes. Invest in a colour wheel and learn how to use it.

Organization

Use a set of drawers, page protectors or other filing system to keep track of all of your paper piecings. Separate them by:

1. Paper piecings that have been bid on/sold but not sent out.
2. Paper piecings that have not been sold.
3. Paper piecings in progress.

You can also have them packed and ready to ship as you list. You may need to combine some paper piecings for a customer that wins multiple pieces, but the packing is already done and makes shipping go faster!

Advertising Your Auction

Do not count on your auctions to advertise themselves! Create an email list and ask every customer if they would like to be notified when you list new auctions. Repeat customers will become some of your best customers.

Keep your email addresses grouped in your address book on your computer and send using the "BCC" so that you are not revealing their email address to anyone. Or use your mailing list on your autoresponder. More on this later.

Profitable New Scrapbooking Business

When you list new auctions, just send out a short email letting them know what you have listed and include a link to your listings page.

You can also send out advertisements on scrapbooking related "groups" or email lists. You can do a search on Yahoogroups.com, the MSN groups or any other email list to find scrapbooking groups. The social networking sites such as MySpace and Facebook also have lots of groups that you can join. Email the list owner to find out what their policies are regarding ads. A lot of lists allow ads to be placed once a week.

There are also "For Sale and Trade" message boards at scrapbooking sites that you can advertise at. I do not recommend advertising on regular message boards, though, because most of them do not allow it and it will really get everyone upset!

Custom Orders

From time to time, you may be contacted by eBay users to create a custom piece for them. This is a good idea as long as you have a commitment from them to buy. You should try to charge right around the same price of the ended auction. Maybe a few dollars short of that. Only do this if you are satisfied with the ending bid price. If the price was too low, feel free to quote a higher price for your work. Be sure to make it worth your time and effort. Do not sell yourself too cheaply!

Profitable New Scrapbooking Business

Here is a sample form letter you can use to reply to custom requests:

---oo---

"Hello! Thank you so much for you interest in placing a custom order for XXXXXXX. I would be willing to make this paper piecing for you for $XXXX plus $XXX for shipping. Please note that insurance is optional and would cost an additional $XXX.

Custom orders may be slightly different than the set you have seen because these items are handmade. Colours may vary slightly also, but I always attempt to get as close to the original as I can.

Please be advised that I am currently allowing XXX days for any custom orders. You can pay for this order using xxx

Please respond to this email to let me know if you still want to order this set. Include your name, address and any special instructions for the paper piecing. Thanks again for your interest!"

---oo---

Undertaking custom orders can be the staple of your business as people who are not necessarily scrapbook talented can provide the illusion that they are – with your help!

Profitable New Scrapbooking Business

Provide Excellent Customer Service

Working with customers through online auction sites is the same as working with any other type of customer. Do your best to provide good customer service. If somebody isn't pleased with an item that they receive, do your best to replace the item or refund the money.

You may want to offer incentive programs to repeat auction even offer to do a free paper piecing after the person wins X amount of your auctions.

Always answer emails in a timely manner, ship items as soon as you receive payment and be polite in all of your correspondence.

When you have a successful auction, be sure to leave feedback for your buyer – but never leave feedback first. Let them leave feedback for you first then reciprocate with them.

Selling paper piecings on eBay can be a very profitable and enjoyable way to build your scrapbooking business. Do your research, and provide the services that people want and need and you will soon build a good reputation on the site.

Target Audience

Whichever type of scrapbooking business you decide to start, you need a group of people to target in order to sell to. This is you market and usually you define this by age group, income level and geographic area. Doing this will help you with your marketing so that you do not market or advertise where your potential buyers are not situated.

You could for example decide to aim for the just married couples who want to scrapbook about their wedding planning, the wedding itself and their honeymoon. This is a good idea because you can then move onto to scrapbooking new babies.

Another way to approach your market is to look at offering evening groups complete with coffee and chat. As you can see this will be a completely different group – possibly the slighter older groups. Lastly you could aim for the retired people who want to scrapbook for their families. Again, this is a different demographic which will have an impact on your marketing, your products and possibly your prices.

Alternatively you might decide to scrapbook for celebrations such as Golden Weddings. Conversely you might just decide to sell supplies or piecings on sites such as eBay.

Profitable New Scrapbooking Business

As you can see, the choices you make in what kind of audience you are seeking, impacts upon the type of business you have, what you sell and where you need to market your services. To give you some thoughts here is a list of possibilities:

Decide first on your mix of products and services you want to offer then look at:
- Celebrations.
- Activities.
- Age group.
- Types of scrapbooks you want to work with.
- General scrapbooking or niche scrapbooks.
- Teaching rather than selling.
- Static or roving business.
- Entertaining with the scrapbooking.
- Groups of people or one by one?

Of course you can always change your mind as your grow your business or you can change the mix of services and products that you want to offer. Whatever audience you aim for it is always better to try and start slowly and with a small budget. You can always get bigger and more adventurous as you become more experienced.

Your Business Kit

This is a business that you can run quite easily from home with just a telephone, a good strong table, some storage and a simple filing system.

Your Brochure

Your brochure can be quickly made up on a PC. Design a one page description of your business and the kind of work that you do. Include your contact details and company name. Do not include too many words – just make it catchy, memorable and informative. You can include a couple of photos of your finished scrapbooks.

If you are unsure as how to produce a brochure, look for a template online or go to a freelance site or design college and ask them to do it for you. The cost should not be too much.

Getting them printed off professionally is far better if you can afford it. Again there are sites on the internet, or your local printer that will do this for you. There are even sites that will both design and print for you. A printed brochure looks far better than one using your home printer.

Profitable New Scrapbooking Business

Business Cards

You should really have a few business cards as well. These can be professionally produced from web sites such as vistaprint or from you local stationary store or printer. These are handy to leave in shops for others to pick up and to hand to potential customers.

Uniform

It would be a good idea to give yourself some kind of uniform such are one of your T shirts or sweaters printed with your company name and one of your great designs.

Match your colours of your uniform and your equipment to your company colours. This makes you look like a professional company. Make sure that everything is cleaned regularly – including your equipment.

Your Sales Pack

Your Sales Pack is the major step in your business – it is what makes your business professional and moves you to the next level. It allows you to work with larger companies or clubs who want to buy your goods in bigger volumes.

The Sales Pack must contain a printout or photocopy of your terms and conditions, insurance and background check, references and your brochure and maybe a business card.

Profitable New Scrapbooking Business

In your terms and conditions you should explain the details of your working policy. This will give information such as: your hours of operation; when a deposit and full payment is due; if you will deliver or not etc. This will make you look organised and professional and also avoid misunderstandings in the future.

Your Equipment

The best thing about scrapbooking is that although there are a plethora of scrapbooking supplies available on the market, you really do not need a lot to make a scrapbook. Basically, all you need to scrapbook is an album, some glue, a pair of scissors, and some photographs or newspaper clippings. Any fabric, ribbon, or bits of leftovers from other projects can be used to embellish the scrapbook. However, professionally, you are going to need more supplies and more variety. As you become busier you are also going to need some professional equipment which will probably be worth the extra cost.

Tools

At the top of this list is an exacto knife. This strong and versatile blade allows you to cut almost anything into any shape. When the blade is dull, the end is simply broken off to reveal another sharp tip. Just be sure to place the object you plan to cut onto a mat or wad or newspaper before using the exacto knife. Otherwise, the knife will cut right through your picture and into the scrapbook page or dining room table.

You might also consider purchasing a professional cutter. When using a cutter, make sure that you have a cutting board underneath to avoid cutting papers underneath or worse putting cut lines on the surface of the table.

Profitable New Scrapbooking Business

In addition to the cushion, cutting boards also have guide lines that will help you cut paper in a straight line.

This will save you a lot of work in sketching and using the ruler just to be able to cut it straight. Cutting boards also have measurements that will help you when you need to cut paper at a certain length.

The plain pair of scissors as well as a pair of pinking shears will be indispensable and you will need to keep them sharp.

The next best tool is a pair of tweezers. Trying to pick up and place small gluey pieces is a hassle. Tweezers, though not very high tech, allow you to move pieces without touching them.

Various glues and affixing options are available. These quick and less messy options include glue dots, two-sided tape, Xyron, acid free photo tabs, and polypropylene corners.

You could also use punches to punch shapes out of paper and these come in shapes of all sizes.

You will also need your cutting tools such as a pair of scissors and cutters, die-cuts, cut-outs etc. Some scrapbookers also use stamps of various sizes and designs.

Rubber stamps can also used and are very versatile such as in card making. They are available in all kinds of shapes and themes.

Albums

There are two standard sizes of albums, the 8.5"x11" and 12"x12". If you are planning to create a family scrapbook, most scrappers will suggest that you use a 12"x12" album because you will need larger space to accommodate all the photos and captions of your family members. If you are creating an album scrapbook for personal use or a scrapbook that you will give as a gift for a loved one, you can use smaller albums such as the 5"x7" album because you can create a very specific theme.

Other specifications of scrapbook albums include the post-bound albums that come with black or white cardstock pages and are covered by sheet protectors. The pages are bound into the album using three posts that enables it to be easily taken out so you can add or remove pages. This kind of album makes it easy for the scrapper to move pages around by pulling the cardstock out of the sheet protector or by sliding in a page where patterned papers are used.

Strap-hinge albums, on the other hand, are those albums that have flexible plastic straps in the cover that run through wire loops embedded in each page.

Profitable New Scrapbooking Business

The 3-ring binders or D-ring binders are albums bound using rings that allow you to add or switch around pages quickly and easily. A 3-ring binder allows you to fit a lot of pages while a D-ring allows the pages in the scrapbook to lie flat.

To increase the preservation of the scrapbook and your treasures, look for albums with acid free, lignin free pages. Both acid and lignin accelerate photo fading and general deterioration. Lignin is a chemical found naturally in the cell walls of plants. If the lignin is not removed in the paper manufacturing process, the chemical will cause the paper product to gradually yellow and crumble. Lignin and acid free products come in virtually any colour and texture.

Paper

Of course you will also need paper. Manufacturers have also made the paper in different shapes and sizes. This gives you the chance of making each scrapbook both memorable and unique. You can buy paper in all shapes, sizes, colours and with many different designs. It is important to decide upon your themes and then buy the appropriate paper.

Embellishments

Scrapbooking involves the use of a lot of materials and supplies such as photos, papers and cardstocks, journaling tools such as pens of various tips and colours, adhesives of all shapes and sizes such as tapes, and glues, embellishments such as buttons, laces, pins, eyelets, patterns, fancy yarns and threads, metal accents, beads, craft wire and fabric ribbon roses that are safely be used on any scrapbook page. You will need a good supply of all of these materials.

You might also consider using chalk or decorative chalks that come in a set with various colours and applicators. They are perfect for shading and highlighting an album page. Then there are eyelets which are great for attaching vellum to paper, for decorating a photo mat or for making a border and which also come in different sizes, colours and shapes.

Storage

Since scrapbooking requires a lot of materials, a scrapper needs a place and space where they can store and carry their materials. There are various products that can help scrapbookers organise their stuff and store their scrapbooks and their scrapbook supplies. Several items include bags or scrapbooking totes where you can put all of your precious scrapbooking materials. These totes can help you keep your photos, tools, stickers, markers, and other supplies from other people's reach.

Profitable New Scrapbooking Business

Aside from bags and scrapbooking totes, another useful means of scrapbooking storage is the scrapbook cases, which usually come in handy and removable snap cases. Here, you can store the scrapbooking supplies and keep them from being lost or damaged. Usually, scrapbook cases are space savers and can perfectly fit into chest-style storage units with a divided top.

You can use this scrapbook case for holding scrapbook pages, photos, stickers, and other scrap-booking tools.

When buying a scrapbook case, make sure that you buy an item which enables you to see the contents inside easy so you can easily identify photos and other materials you wish to use. Since you will be putting photos inside the scrapbook case, make sure that it is acid and PVC free.

In the market, there are various scrapbook cases available which enables you to transport, organise, and protect 25 to 75 pieces of 12x12 pages or photos.

The scrapbook organiser, on the other hand, is a very practical and sensible scrapbook storage solution. They usually come with different pockets where you can neatly organise the scrapbook papers, stamps, stickers, markers, and other supplies in its handy and easy-to-remove snap cases. Scrapbook organisers are a must for a scrapbooker who is always on the go because it can help you keep all of your supplies in one place.

Scrapbook organisers can be folded into half for easy transport with wide shoulder strap or carrying handle for east use.

In looking for a scrapbook case or scrapbook organiser, make sure that you look for those that can fit neatly into a chest-style storage unit and those that occupy minimal space in your office or craft room. Also, look for scrapbook organisers with features such as divided areas that are perfect for drawing utensils such as paintbrushes and pencils.

Office Kit

You should also have one or more message boards in your office to hold both messages and design ideas you have found. If you are holding classes and seminars, you might also find a wall planner very useful.

You will also need an accountancy package or MsExcel to keep your accounts and MsWord for your invoices/receipts and correspondence. Email will make your customer correspondence quicker and easier for both you and your customers.

Some scrappers use computer based graphics to enhance their work so you might like to investigate various graphic software packages. Obviously you will also need a good quality colour printer.

Storage And Inventory Control

When you are running your business you will want to have enough space in your office to accommodate your products. Organisational skills are at a premium here. You will want plenty of shelf space to store papers, die cuts, albums, stamps and stickers as well as your rulers, scissors and other equipment.

Spending time digging through drawers and boxes looking for supplies is frustrating and time consuming and time is money. There are simple and inexpensive ways to help you spend less time searching for your supplies and more time exactly creating.

Sorting supplies by categories or themes is very useful and you can tell at a glance what you have in stock. Some useful categories are winter, Christmas, Easter, Valentines, Baby girl, Baby boy, etc. Plastic boxes or baskets are a great way of storing your kit. Get a few in the same size so that you can stack them and they look tidy in your office. Create labels using 2"x 4" address labels and your computer so that you can quickly find your stock.

Place fibres and ribbons in small plastic bags and store them in your theme containers. Smaller plastic containers work great to store fibres by colours. You can also use recycled clear jars, cleaned and labels removed, and sort by colour. Add your labels to these also.

Profitable New Scrapbooking Business

Photo boxes are a great size for holding spools of ribbon and these come in clear also. Another great solution is to hang a pretty curtain rod on your wall and thread those ribbon spools on the curtain rod.

Paper is one of the most important staples and storage is also a major problem for most at home scrap booking businesses. Paper comes in hundreds of different colours, patterns, textures and weights. It needs to be kept dry and clean, be photo safe and stored in plain sight.

Paper can be stored in a wide variety of ways but horizontal is the best. There are lots of wonderful products out there, from wire storage racks to clear stacking plastic trays and are very good investments.

You'll also want to start some sort of inventory control system so you always know what you have on hand at any given time. This does not have to be a complicated task. Start an Excel spreadsheet and update it every time you make a sale. Either keep it on your computer or it you are not so comfortable with that, print it off and keep it on a clipboard. For those less technical a set of small file cards in a file box is another option.

Work in progress can be kept in larger boxes so that they are stored without creasing or bending.

Pricing Your Services

Pricing is so important to the success of your business. You are in a very competitive business and you will be judged on your prices compared with your competitors. However if you are clever you will build yourself a niche and people will look to you for that particular service.

When pricing the scrapbook or any scrapping products that you wish to sell you should take into consideration the following costs:

- Buying your products wholesale, including delivery costs or the cost of picking them up.
- Your consumables such as paper, books, ribbons, glue, tape etc.
- Any design costs, licences etc.
- A percentage of your equipment that you use such as cutters, printers, computer, software etc.
- A percentage of any retail space costs that you might have. If you work from home, a percentage of your office costs.
- If you are running seminars, courses or events then the total costs of setting up and running these should be calculated and then divided by the number of people that you expect to attend.

As with all pricing, you should include a reasonable profit element. You should set some money aside to build up your brand image by advertising and training any staff or distributors that you may have.

A Successful Business Start up

Right you have sorted out your business ideas, you are ready to go ahead and you know what you want to sell and to whom. Now you need your business structure. These are all the things that make up your business. They include:

- **Legal Base:** This includes such factors as your licenses, insurances and setting up your company.
- **Your Market:** You need to decide who you want to market your services to and where they will be.
- **Your Services:** You now need to decide what services you are going to offer to these people, how you would like to package them and what prices you wish to charge.
- **Your Business Plan:** Whether you are looking for funding or not – a business plan is the foundation of a new business.
- **Your Funding:** You should now take your business plan and look around for funding, starting with your Bank.
- **Your Premises:** Look around for your new premises, preferably in the middle of your potential market. Remember that central to your success is the position you choose for your business. Foot traffic past your door and many potential customers within a short journey from

your new business is vital to you finding customers.

- **Web Site:** Most businesses have them now – so even if you do not want to set one up now – at least buy and hold onto your domain name – in case someone else gets hold of it.
- **Your Staff:** Good staff that reflect your business ideals are vital so spend some time spend some time finding the best staff you can.
- **Marketing:** So important and so difficult to get right. Start with a good marketing strategy and go from there.
- **Grand Opening:** Make sure you make a splash and attract as much curiosity as possible.

Your Business Framework

When starting a business of what ever kind, large or small, there is a always a require framework or scaffolding that you have to set up. Not only does this make your business much more effective, but it also saves you from a lot of embarrassing and costly problems. When you start up your business, remember to tick off the 10 items below and you will have a very sound start to your business. Here is your framework:

- **Business Name.** Choose an appropriate name that sums up what your business stands for. It has to be unique – try and ensure that a suitable domain name is also available as you will probably want a web site as well. The owner of an established web site might cause problems if you give your brick based business the same name – so be careful in your choice.
- **Your Business Entity.** Obtain professional advice as whether to the best way to set up your business as a limited company, partnership etc. Then register your company.
- **Patents and** Trademarks. If you have unique products then you need to ensure that you have registered your patents before your start trading. Similarly any product names, mottos, selling tags etc should be trademarked. Take professional advice on how to do this.

- **Licenses and Permits.** Ensure that you have all the licenses and permits that you are legally required to have.
- **Insurance.** You may think that you do not need this but you do and will. So take out property, business, vehicle liability, staff and disaster insurance. A good broker can advise you.
- **Taxes.** A necessary evil I am afraid. Register with your local tax collector. Set up a good accounting system and hire a good accountant.
- **Employment Laws.** Establish what you local employment laws are and ensure that you adhere to them. Set up employee guidelines and handbooks. Make sure you hire and fire legally.
- **Banking.** Visit your local banks and find the best business bank account and credit card for you business. Always keep your business and personal spending separate.
- **Business Plan.** This is your carefully written plan on how you want your company to operate, what you want to sell, where and to whom. It includes your business and marketing strategy as well as your financial standing and projections. This is the foundation of your business.
- **Liquid Cash.** Ensure that you have enough money to carry your through the first few months of your business as well as any foreseeable troublesome times ahead.

The Nasties

Tax, Insurance and Licences these are the nasties of your business and all of them are compulsory! Look up your local state/county/country web site to see what licences you will need. Similarly your country's tax web site will tell you what taxes you will need to pay, how you register to pay them and what forms you will need to fill in to become legal. Do not attempt to work without them – there goes the way to a world of misery. Tax officials in particular, are trained to find and collect unpaid taxes and these are always combined with extra costs and penalties.

Operating your business in some countries will require you and your staff to be licensed before you can start work. This should be displayed on your premises or available for view by your customers.

You may also need a sales tax permit (USA and other sales tax based countries) or VAT registration (UK and some Europe and Asia) if you reach the VAT registration limit.

It would also be advisable to have a background check if this is available. You should also obtain the appropriate insurance if you are opening a retail area or working in people's homes or premises. It would also be good to have at least two checkable references. Once you have all of these you should take photocopies of these and put them together in your Sales Pack.

Check List For Starting A New Business

You are ready to give up your job to start your new business, or even scarier, sink your savings into your new business. You just want to make sure that you have done everything possible to succeed; here is a check list for you.

1. Legal Stuff:
   - Do you have a memorable business name and the associated domain name?
   - Do you have a legal name and business entity?
   - Have you got all your licences?
   - Have you got all you certificates such as fire?
   - Have you registered everything you need to?
   - Have you told the tax department and got your numbers and details?
   - Are all your shares, statutory meetings etc. correct?
   - Do you have all your patents and trademarks?
   - Do you have the legal documents on your premises – leases, sales, mortgages etc.?
   - Do you have all the posters and legal manuals etc that you need?

2. Strategies and Planning:
   - Do you have your Business Plan written?
   - Do you have a Business Strategy?
   - Do you have a Marketing Strategy?
   - Have you decided upon what Business Model you will use?

3. Protection:
    - Do you have your insurances for you, the company, liabilities, staff, premises and vehicles?
    - Have you got health insurance for you and staff if necessary?
    - Do you have your pension set up?

4. Finances:
    - Are your finances in place and have you signed all the forms necessary?
    - Do you have enough and on the right terms?
    - Have you got your bank set up?
    - Do you have your credit/debit card and payment processor set up?

5. Premises:
    - Are your premises/office ready and equipped?
    - Are all the utilities that you need connected – gas, electric, phone, broadband etc.?
    - Do you have all the vehicles, computers and machinery that you need?

6. Staff:
    - Do you have all the staff you need?
    - Are they trained or ready to be trained?
    - Do you have the necessary uniforms?

7. Marketing and Products:
    - Have you checked who your potential market is and where these customers are hiding?
    - Have you ensured that what you are selling is really, really what your proposed customers want?
    - Do you have your pricing and upgrading sorted out?
    - Do you have your branding sorted out?
    - Do you have your starting marketing materials?
    - Do you have standard replies to customer enquiries, invoices, receipts, business cards and letter heads sorted out?

How Much Does It Cost To Start A Business?

You've got your business idea, think that you will be able to get a good loan and even have your business plan being written but.... The one big burning issue is – How much does it cost to start a business?

Well you first of all have to be realistic and understand that you are unlikely to make a profit within the first six months of business – so you should also budget for your first six months running costs. So here is your shopping list:

1) **Purchase or rental of lease/franchise/premises.** This will include any Realtor fees, deposits and other legal expenses. Even small businesses need some kind of premises. To start with you can use a home office, but you are going to need somewhere to hold all that stock and materials that you will soon need as you get bigger. If you intend to only rent somewhere then take into account any deposit you will need as well as at least six month's rental costs.

2) **Cost of fit out and purchase of new equipment.** This will include any work that needs to be done on your premises as well as any equipment you have to buy in order to start and run your business. Often you can lease equipment in order to mitigate high start up costs. This also includes a car or van to deliver your stock to your distributors.

3) **Six months worth of advertising and marketing**. This will be particularly high at the start as you establish your business. Factor in some cold calling as well as a launch party or opening day. Marketing will include a lot of local advertising in order to attract good distributors.

4) **Legal, licensing and banking costs.** Your business will need to be set up correctly, licensed and have a good bank account. Sadly all of these require money. You may also need a payment processing service to use credit cards.

5) **Staff costs for six months.** Staff will be the basis of providing good service to your new customers. Make sure that you have enough money put aside to find them, train them and keep them! Much of your staff costs will be on a commission basis but you will still require admin staff and one or two "on staff" distributors and maybe warehouse staff as well. They will all want to be paid, often before you get paid for your sales.

6) **Uniforms, office and marketing supplies, packaging etc**. You will need to establish your brand. This means that your staff will need uniforms or at the least business cards and name tags. You will need brochures, adverts etc. If appropriate you will also need standardised packaging and documentation.

Your office will also need office equipment and supplies. You should also budget for designing your logo, brochures and adverts if you cannot do this yourself.

Profitable New Scrapbooking Business

7) **Stock and supplies** – to keep you going for six months. This is a big expense because if you have 10 hosts they all need a core stock from which to sell from.

8) **Maintenance** for six months – your equipment will also need to keep going for six months. This includes your cars, computers, printers, copiers etc. Budget for a lot of printing ink!

9) **Any loans** that you have will also have to be paid. Again look at least at six months or until you break even and can pay the loan.

10) **Your salary** for six months – lastly you will need to pay your own bills and maintain your family during this time. You should expect that for a short while your standard of living will go down.

Add this up and add 10% for contingency and some good luck.

Profitable New Scrapbooking Business

Check List – Business Start Up Costs

Purchase/Rental of lease/franchise/premises	√
Realtor /Agent Fees	
Legal Fees	
Bank Fees	
Payment Processing Fees	
Business Consultancy Fees	
Business Planning Fees	
Deposits	
Business Equipment	
Manufacturing Equipment	
Office Equipment –fax, computer etc.	
Stock	
Office Stock – stationary, etc.	
Vehicle Detailing or sign writing	
Property Sign Writing	
Electric/Gas/Water/Phones	
Telecoms and internet	
Maintenance, Leasing and Hiring Fees	
Advertising and Marketing Costs	
Marketing Brochures, Business Cards etc.	
Design Costs	
Staff Costs	
Staff Uniforms	
Training	
Salary Costs	

Will I Succeed?

You've got a great idea, you are pretty sure that what you have will sell; you have even got some cash together. Have you got what it will take to succeed? What else do you need?

Vision: You must be able to see where you are going and what the future will hold. See what others are not able to see and build your business on these visions.

Courage: The ability to act upon your vision despite having doubts. Having the courage to give up job security and a planned future for the opportunity of a successful new business.

Strategy: Having the courage to act upon your vision, you now need to build your strategies. You will need a business and a marketing strategy. These are the formulas that you will use to drive forward and manage your business.

Planning Skills: To ensure that you reach your vision, you need copious amounts of planning. Planning how you will reach your targets, how you will meet new changes and challenges and how you will improve your business. You will need a business plan and a marketing plan.

Researching: Having decided what your business is going to be, then you will need to find out who will want to buy from your business and at what price. This takes a fair amount of researching.

Conceptualising: Knowing what you want to sell and to whom, you now need to define your products and services. Brainstorm different things that you associate with your company. Include everything, good and bad, until you are out of ideas. Keep in mind that ideas generate ideas. Write everything down, this is how you move your company forward. Use this period to design your products, what you want your company to look like and how you want it to be perceived by your customers.

Creativity: You will need the ability to think outside of the box. Keep ahead of your competitors by coming up with new, unusual and unique concepts and solutions to their needs. You will need to create marketing materials, packaging and sales pitches – all will need verbal and visual creativity.

Determination: Along the way you will come across many hurdles and set backs, you will need to dig deep, make your changes and keep going. Determination and the belief in your visions and plans will keep you on the road to success.

Humour: When the entire world seems against you and all seems to be going wrong, when your customers seem to be your worst enemy then you need a sense of humour to carry you forward.

Lastly you need good luck!

Getting Started With Little Money

The age old question, you want to start your business but have little capital available. So how do you do it?

First of all have a look round for sources of borrowing money. The first obvious step is your bank. They are unlikely to lend money unless you have at least a deposit of 20%. Similarly if you approach the Small Business Bureau (USA) or Small Business Association (UK) or similar and ask for a guaranteed loan – they are probably going to want a similar deposit.

They may be able to offer you some advice as to where to go for funding. Your best bet is to get together a realistic business plan with what you wish to do and what it will cost in quite detailed format. Also include details of whom you expect your market to be and how large this market is.

A venture capitalist or angel investor is pretty much out of the question unless you have a really unique protected product or a very well established business.

Another source of business funding help may be to apply for a grant. They are difficult to get and you will have to have, not only a good case but a very well defined business idea.

Profitable New Scrapbooking Business

So if you are capital poor the best advice is to start small. Look at a smaller version of what you intend to start up. Start with offering your services to local businesses first and working from a home office. Start selling from a mall kart or stall in a flea market, boot sale or local market place. You can also try eBay, CraigsList etc.

Start small and you have not risked too much. Build your business, establish your business name and build up capital and customers then you are in a much better position to seek funding.

What Goes Into A Business Plan?

You are ready to write your business plan for funding purposes, or you are starting a new business and know that you need one. So what goes into your business plan?

Well first of all, a good, well structured business plan can be the foundation to your new company. It is important that you spend some time ensuring that it is accurate. Here are the relative portions of your business plan.

- **Executive Summary**. This will be the first thing read by your potential investor and a strong executive summary with an overview of all that is required will ensure that the rest of your business plan is read.
- **Business Overview** and structure including shares issued and who owns them. This is where you describe your physical business, your business model, your Mission Statement, objectives of the business and key milestones,
- **Business Strategies** including business, financial, marketing and exit strategy. This is an important part of your business plan and details how you are going to mange your future business. The business strategy is how you run your business and how you intend to expand and grow from a new business. The financial strategy is how you will manage your finances, when you

Profitable New Scrapbooking Business

will invest, how much will go into research, if you will lease or buy etc.

Profitable New Scrapbooking Business

Your marketing strategy deals with marketing and advertising your business, to whom, how and at what costs. Your exit strategy is how the investor will be able to recoup their investment.

- **Markets**, which is who you expect to buy your products and services with some predictions of volumes.
- **Products**, which are the services and goods offered. You should include how they are manufactured or sourced as well as the fulfilment process.
- **Financials** such as costs, overheads, profit etc with realistic indications of why, how and when. You should also include your marketing and staffing budgets as well as overhead costs and your break even position.
- **Staffing** including resumes/CV's of major staff, brief terms of reference and an organisation chart.
- **The Way Forward**, what will happen in the future and how an investor will get their money back.

If you include all of these you will have a great business plan. This can seem daunting, which is why it can be worthwhile to employ a business planning consultant, who can also provide business consultancy. Good luck.

Meeting The Bank Manager

Meeting with your bank to ask for a loan for your business is always going to be a challenge even if you have a profitable business. Here are a few ideas for you.

It is important to remember that your loan manager is probably a kind human being who has to adhere to the bank's rules on lending. The basic ones are:

- That you can repay the loan.
- The loan is for a reasonable business reason.
- That your business is viable and bona fida business.

Go to the meeting armed with:

- Your business details such as licenses etc.
- An outline of your business and how you see it expanding in the next few years.
- Your business plan.
- How much money you require and when you need it.
- How you will spend it and on what items.
- How your business will benefit or expand with the loan.
- What collateral you can offer the bank but do not offer this until asked.
- When and how you will repay the loan.

Try not to hide anything – evasion is not a good reflection on your business acumen. If you are asked a difficult question then answer it as honestly as you can – but by putting a good spin so that you sound positive.

Some Scrapbooking Themes

Scrapbooking is a wonderful and creative means to be able to preserve memories and share them with other people. A scrapbook should be a visual and tactile delight, showcasing photographs along with other "scraps" or bits and pieces of something that when put together tells a complete story of that particular slice of life depicted in the particular photo.

For instance, a photograph of a person hardly tells a story especially if the photo has no other particular merits or characteristics other than it containing a face. Creatively making a layout of it in a scrapbook allows you to tell the story behind the photograph. By adding other elements from different mediums, you can explain the photograph and the memory behind it without using something as blatant as actual statements.

The challenge of scrapbooking is in being able to utilise various elements to enhance a photograph while being limited to a finite area. Sometimes, in our zeal to tell a story, we tend to clutter and create a busy layout for our scrapbook. Perhaps it is important to remember that when we do scrapbooking, the inclusion of "scraps" or other creative elements into a layout is done to enhance a photo and tell a story that the photograph simply cannot do on its own. The layout of the elements incorporated should not take away from the photograph.

Profitable New Scrapbooking Business

A good guideline is to maintain a clean and simple layout for scrapbook projects. A clean and simple layout may be more manageable to create and maintain. This means that you incorporate more synergy and symmetry in your layout instead of a haphazard collection of images, textures and colours.

One of the reasons that people do scrapbooks is because they want to preserve the memories of some great occasion or event. In fact, a scrapbook has long been synonymous with albums because it is primarily filled with pictures and memories. One difference with an album and a scrapbook is the fact that you can put a whole lot more in a scrapbook than just photos.

You can place three-dimensional objects that make the occasion more memorable and meaningful. Below are some occasions that people often create a scrapbook for.

Coming of a Baby

An ordinary baby album will probably contain the baby's first photos but a scrapbook can contain not only the first photos but also some of the special milestones that the baby will go through in their first year. All the firsts that they will experience in their life can be documented in a scrapbook.

Profitable New Scrapbooking Business

For instance, you can include the baby's strands of hair after he gets their first cut. You can bind these and then place in a piece of see-through plastic. Another first are the nails that were first cut, both from the fingers of the hands and the feet. Parents can also include copies of special documents such as the birth certificate and the baptismal certificate. Another great idea is to put the baby's thumbprint, handprint and foot print. Some will also paste a piece of the baby's first ultrasound photo, their first medical certificate and their first vaccination chart.

Wedding and Wedding Anniversaries

A wedding scrapbook may contain pictures at the wedding but it can also include wrappers from the gifts of the guests, wishes that the guests gave for the newlyweds and the gift cards that they have put on their gifts. This is one way to preserve the day not only for the newlyweds but also for their guests.

Another good idea is to document not only the wedding itself but also the days or months of preparation for the wedding. Photos can capture events like the bachelor's party, the bridal shower and even the pre-wedding practice.

The scrapbook may also contain the invitation for the wedding, dried flowers from the bouquet of the bride, a piece of the garter, mayhap even the souvenir if one can manage to paste it on the scrapbook.

Graduation

Another event that is worthy of reminiscing is the graduation. This marks the ending and the beginning of an old and a new chapter in a person's life. A graduation scrapbook can contain the invitation for the event, the investiture that is usually given to the graduates, some pieces of strings from the tussles, and of course the photos of the graduates. Corsages that are dried may also be put in the scrapbook if one can find a way to paste it in a flat surface.

If you can, you can also include messages from the graduate's classmates and friends as well as to his or her teachers. Put the messages in a kind of message board. If there are awards merited, one can put the medals or copies of the certificates in the scrapbook. If the graduate did a special address, a copy of the speech should also be included in the scrapbook.

Themes can also be personalized to the scrapbook recipient's special interests. Special interests themes include favourite colours, sports, favourite television programmes, music, the outdoors, or cultural influences. When seeking a theme ask three questions:
- What is the overall purpose for the scrapbook?
- Who is the scrapbook for?
- Who is the scrapbook about?

The answers to these three questions are all factors in selecting an appropriate theme. For instance, the scrapbook a medical school graduate is probably completely different than a grandparent book. The student will probably appreciate a scrapbook with photographs, poems and journals. Perhaps, the theme of the scrapbook could be medicine. You could create embellishments that looked like scalpels and tweezers around various pictures of the student during his college years? A scrapbook for a man would be totally different to that of a woman.

Whichever type of scrapbook you decide to produce, the theme is very important and you need to decide upon this before you start work on a scrapbook.

Title

Do not forget to create a title for the scrapbook page. Though adding a title might seem to be obvious or unimportant, a title defines the whole basis of the scrapbook. The title instantly tells the viewer what the page is all about. In one word or one short phrase, the title tells the reader the theme and purpose of the scrapbook.

Titles can be as basic as the date of an event, the name of an individual, or a specific event.

Titles can also be more interesting and exciting. These can include quotes, sayings, fillers, or simple phrases. The best places to look for title inspiration are in greeting cards, advertisements, and commercials.

Colour

Colour coordination and contrast will highlight and accent the scrapbook. A well thought out colour scheme can help define the theme of a page, attract attention to specific items, or detract away from mistakes. Poorly chosen colour schemes, on the other hand, can cause the scrapbook page to look gaudy or mismatched.

Background colours can be matched, coordinated, or contrasted with the colours in your photographs, mementos, or embellishments. Matching colours add to the continuity of the colour scheme. Coordinated colours add depth to scrapbook pages. Contrasted colours focus the eye. In this way, colour can be used to create the effect you desire.

A great way to see how colours look together is to collect and compare colour wheels from your local paint or hardware store. Paint wheels are usually available free for the taking in nearly any paint department.

Scrapbooking Tips

Even the most experienced scrapbooker can do with some help sometimes, so here are some tips that you might not know.

Photographs

Most scrapbooks will contain photographs. Even the most disinterested reader of the scrapbook will glance at the photographs. Pictures really are worth a thousand words. Therefore, it is important to choose photographs that are of good quality and clearly illustrate the scrapbook theme.

Any photograph can be used in a scrapbook. Even instant photographs can be used in scrapbooking. Just be careful that the chemicals within the photograph do not spill out on the rest of the scrapbook. Digital pictures can easily be printed right onto lignin-free and acid -free paper.

Always keep in mind that scrapbooking is permanent. Therefore, it is probably preferable to use copies of the only picture of Great Grandma rather than risk ruining the photograph forever. Simply scan the picture on your computer scanner and print the image on lignin free and acid free paper.

Cutting and Cropping

Often photographs aren't quite the right shape and size or the photographic image is improperly cantered. Having oversized or off cantered photographs creates an air of unprofessionalism. Carefully cropped and sized photographs, on the other hand, enhances the overall look and feel of the scrapbook.

There are two ways to solve these problems. The low tech way to solve these problems are to manually crop and shape the photograph using a pair of scissors or an exacto knife. If you are manually cropping and cutting pictures, make sure that you mark the outline you want with chalk (or eye shadow if you do not have chalk) before you cut. Remember the old saying, measure twice and cut once.

To manually change a distracting or cluttered background simply cut out the background and replace it with a with a new paper background. This allows the eye to focus on the people instead of the clutter behind them.

The high tech solution to your photograph woes is to use modern computer programmes such as Photo Editor. Using these programmes, photographs can be magically darkened, brightened, sharpened, enlarged, and cropped without ruining your original photograph. Some programmes even allow you to change the background of the photograph.

Order

There are no specific rules stating that all photographs or mementos must be placed in chronological order. Therefore, it is completely up you the order you wish to place your items and embellishments. You can place your items in a formal chronological order. You can also group items into formal or informal categories such as similar colours, events, activities, individuals, or families. Items can also be placed into random, abstract, or collages.

Each order has its own place in scrapbooking. For instance, chronological order might be useful for an anniversary scrapbook. Pictures and mementos of the couple's years together could be placed from the first day they met through the wedding day to the present day with each time period on a different page. This presents a feel of as time goes by.

However, a scrapbook for a parent might just have a collage of pictures and drawings. In this case, a collage lends to a feeling of overwhelmingly being loved.

Text

You may or may not want to add text to the scrapbook page. You may want to just write captions below the pictures. You may want to add your own stories or poems. You may want to add journals describing the day to day life of your baby or your child's accomplishments. Text can be used as either a focal point or simply as a supporting piece.

Text may be hand written. Alternately, computer fonts, letters, text, or three-dimensional images can also be printed or cut and pasted onto the page. In this way, various styles, colours, textures, and visual text effects are possible.

Tags

Tags are a little added touch of professionalism that adds to the overall well thought out look to the scrapbook. Tags can be used for accents, captions, and thought bubbles as well as dedications. The design of your tags will depend entirely on your personal needs and desires. Thus, tags can be big or small, square or specially shaped, white or coloured, plain or textured.

Furthermore, tags need not be made of paper. Some of the most interesting tags are made from fabric, wood, and furniture odds and ends found around the house. Be creative. Pre-made tags are available at most craft or office supply stores.

Embellishments

Your own unique embellishments add a special personal touch to the scrapbook pages. Embellishments can be used as the main focus of your page, to highlight items, or as borders. Embellishments can range from simple items such as stickers and ribbon to more complex techniques such as adding faux beads and silver accenting. Use your imagination and creativity.

Embellishments need not be expensive. Odds and ends that you have from other craft projects work just fine. Be on the lookout for sales on fabric, plastic flowers, lace, beads, and whatever else takes your fancy. These items will no doubt come in handy on your next scrapbook project. Also keep a sharp eye out for deals in second hand stores and garage sales. Often used items can be ripped apart and the pieces reused literally for only pennies.

Patterning

How can you arrange the scrapbook page to best show off the mementos and embellishments? You can place everything in the centre of the page, place a single focus item in the centre, or divide the page into sections adding items to each section. You may also choose to lay the items out in a standard recipe or calendar layout.

Shapes also make interesting placement patterns. Common shapes include circles, squares, hearts, and stars. However, you can also place items in object patterns such as mountains, trains, or Christmas trees.

The shape you choose for the scrapbook will depend entirely on your theme. For instance, a logical shape for a wedding or Valentines Day scrapbook is a heart. A nice shape for a Christmas scrapbook is a Christmas tree. You might make a cake pattern for you niece the pastry cook. Let your imagination and creativity be your guide. Various ready made patterning templates are available on the market.

Spacing

Spacing is a difficult matter. There is a fine line between having a balanced scrapbook page and a gaudy mess. If items are too closely spaced your reader will feel overwhelmed. If your items are spaced to far apart your viewer will feel short changed.

- Look at your page.
- Close your eyes.
- Open them again.
- Does your page look cluttered?
- Does your page have more photographs than background?
- Are your embellishments drawing the focus away from your mementos?

Then, you need to simplify your page a bit and increase the spacing between objects. Remember you can always add more pages.

- Is your page bare?
- Is your page uninteresting and colourless?

Then, think about adding some more mementos and colourful embellishments. In this way, you can decrease the spacing between objects making your page more energetic.

Mounting

Once the scrapbooking page is laid out to your liking you can begin attaching and gluing your various mementos, text, and titles. Never glue as you go! Not only will glue end up all over the place but you will no doubt find out too late that the title doesn't go well with the photograph or that the spacing is too tight.

There are several ways to attach items to the scrapbook page. Some of the best sanity savers include glue dots, glue pens, Xyron adhesives, and two-sided tape. Glue dots and glue are fairly mess free and stick to almost anything made of paper or fibre. Mini glue dots are great for those very small items. Xyron adhesives and two-sided tape works for those larger jobs and work on almost any item type.

Getting Rid of Messes and Mistakes

No matter how careful you are, you will undoubtedly find a mistake, mark, or mess on your finished scrapbook page. If you find a mistake, mark or glue bits on the scrapbook page, just rub it off using a soft white eraser. Alternately, make the mark into an interesting squiggle or doodle. For mistakes in journal text, cover the mistake with a sticker the same colour as the journal page. Then, just write over the sticker. White out can also be used for white pages. Fingerprint smudges on your photographs can be removed by rubbing the fingerprints with a piece of flannel or a dry baby wipe.

Profitable New Scrapbooking Business

Excess powder or glitter can be brushed away. This is time consuming and frustrating. The best solution is to reduce static electricity before you add the powder or glitter. Just place a drier sheet on top of the page before you work.

Preservation

You put a great deal of time, thought, and effort into the scrapbook pages. Therefore, you should try to protect and preserve your work.

The most important way to protect your pages is by using lignin free and acid free products. Lignin free and acid free protects will reduce yellowing and crumbling. Also, use coloured paper or ink that is resistant to fading due to age, exposure to light, heat, and other unfavourable conditions.

To protect your page from the outside world, use Mylar or page protectors. Special page protectors for three-dimensional pages are also available at most craft stores. These protection pages not only protect your objects but also reduce indentations caused by three-dimensional objects.

Newspaper Clippings

A popular addition to scrapbook pages is newspaper clippings. Newspaper clippings of birth announcements, team photographs, or favourite celebrities add a personal touch to scrapbook pages.

Newspaper contains about 4% lignin. Therefore, yellowing and brittleness of the newspaper paper will eventually occur. However, since the percentage of lignin is low, newspaper will preserve for many years before this deterioration process begins to occur. To further slow this process, use Mylar or page protectors to protect the newspaper from the outside elements.

Graphics and Clipart

Various graphics and clip art are available on the Internet. Many of these items can be downloaded or printed for free. Downloading and printing images is a good way to find pictures or photographs of your child's favourite television character or band for a unique personalized touch. Print these graphics or clipart directly onto lignin-free and acid-free paper.

Weaving Photographs

For more dramatic results from your photographs, trying weaving two copies of the same photograph together. This technique creates a three-dimensional artist look. This technique would look great on a scrapbook for a graduating art student or a scrapbook for a friend who is quite artist and creative. This technique might also look good on a child's scrapbook with a kid's art background giving the whole page an abstract look.

Profitable New Scrapbooking Business

To achieve this technique, first you need two copies of the same photo. On one photograph, draw evenly spaced vertical lines on the back of the picture. Cut along these lines with scissors or an exacto knife. On the other photograph draw and cut along evenly spaced horizontal lines.

Next, using alternate strips, from photograph one and then photograph two, weave the pieces together. To preserve the rectangular shape of the photographs, start your weaving in the centre of the piece and work outwards.

Collage

Collages are congregations of photographs or news clippings. These items can be placed in any order or pattern. Collages can have a theme such as a single individual or an entire family group combined.

Collages create great funky scrapbook pages. This method is especially useful for surprise scrapbooks meant to overwhelm the reader either with all of their accomplishments or all those that care for them.

In addition to photographs and news clippings, collages can also contain blocks of text or embellishment. These additions can be used to increase the busyness and overwhelming nature of the collage or reduce the effect slightly by distracting the focus away from the collage.

To reduce shifting of the photographs as you select an appropriate collage design, place temporary tape on each photograph or newspaper clipping. Once the display is set, start permanently attaching the collage to the background.

Photograph Mosaics

An attractive technique for placing photographs into scrapbooks is the photograph mosaic. Mosaics stretch photographs into an artistic rendition of the original photograph. Maps can also be stretched in this way. This method might be employed to create a funky look for a friend scrapbook or as a background for someone who likes computers, GIS, or geography.

A basic cropping technique is used to create a photographic mosaic. Simply cut a photograph into evenly spaced squares. Then, glue the squares onto the background leaving an equal space between each square.

A white background or a background matching the background colour of the photograph will add to the effect. A background of a contrasting colour will reduce the spaced out effect of the photograph.

Markers

A marker is a seeming obvious tool for writing and embellishing on scrapbook pages. Markers are easy to draw with and can be used to colour in portions of lettering, in borders, or to create accents.

Unfortunately, regular markers tend to smudge and bleed through scrapbook pages.

Nonetheless, there are a few brands of markers (Markers Pigma and Colour Workshop Blo Pens) available in craft and office supply stores that do not smudge or bleed. These markers are also acid free, fade resistant, waterproof, and available in a variety of colours.

Wax Pencils

Another important writing implement for scrapbooking is a wax pencil. Wax pencils are soft pencils designed to write on glass, plastic and photographs. These pencils are easy to draw with and can be used to colour in portions of lettering, in borders, or to create accents.

The unique thing about wax pencils is that if they are used on the front of a photograph, the ink will rub off. However, when used on the back of a photograph, the ink will become permanent. Wax pencil ink is acid free and available in a variety of colours.

Stickers

Stickers are fun and easy to stick to scrapbook pages. Stickers can be used for captions, thought bubbles, to hide mistakes, or as embellishments. Stickers of your child's favourite cartoon or television programme can add a personal accent to the scrapbook page.

However, not all stickers are suitable for scrapbooking. Check to see if the stickers are lignin free and acid free. Furthermore, be careful that the sticker adhesive does not dry out or seep around the edges. Never place a sticker on a photograph as the adhesive may cause irreversible damage to the photograph.

Rubber Stamping

Rubber stamps dipped in acid free ink can be used to create various embellishments. Rubber stamps can be used to create cute images for children's and grandparents scrapbooks. They can also be simple flowers or leaves to create elegant looks for gift scrapbooks.

Furthermore, these embellishments can be used to focus on a certain photograph or memento. Alternately, these embellishments can be used to soften the look of a busy or sharp image. One low cost alternative to the rubber stamp is a cotton ball. This creates a shadowy effect.

Another alternative is to buy the pads and attach them to furniture castors. The thick caster allows you to position the stamp in exactly the right place. Moreover, attaching the stamp to a wider base allows you to press more evenly on the stamp. This creates a complete and evenly balanced stamp every time.

Faux Wax Seals

A good way to make your own personal seals is with Crayola Model Magic. Simply, roll out a small ball of the clay. Then, imprint this ball with a small rubber stamp or a brass seal. In this way, you can create whatever stamp impressions you can imagine.

Tearing

As the word suggests, tearing is the ripping of paper or tissue paper into various shapes or abstract forms. Tearing creates an artist look to backgrounds, borders, and embellishments. Be aware however, because tearing does not comply well with all themes. In some more formal themes tearing appears unprofessional.

Fraying

Fraying can create extremely interesting and artist border accents. Fraying looks especially good in children's scrapbooks, as well as pages for your more creative and imaginative friends. Be careful, fraying does not comply well with all themes. In some more formal themes fraying creates an unprofessional appearance.

Just cut your paper border about an inch larger than you need. Then, dampen this border by dipping only the edges of the paper into a shallow dish of water. Then, the edges of the paper can then be easily pulled off.

Curled Edges

For a unique look to your background and borders, curl the edges of your border and background pages. Curled edges give depth to a scrapbook page. Furthermore, curled edges can soften and reduce the focus of a busy scrapbook page by directing the eye outwards.

To create a curled look, simply wet one edge of the border or background paper. Next, using your fingers, manipulate the paper into a curl. This curled edge can then be left as is, chalked, or inked for a more dramatic effect.

Antique Look

An antique look can increase the dramatic impact of your theme or add a feeling of wisdom and age to the scrapbooking page. Adding an antique look to your background or journals can be accomplished in several ways. One way is to simple wrinkle cardstock. Another way is to scratch the paper with an emery board or sandpaper. Your antique page can then be left as is, chalked, or inked for an even more dramatic effect.

Leather Look

A leather look can add elegance to the scrapbooking page. To create a unique leather look, simply distress cardstock. To do this, grip the cardstock in your hands. Then, with a gentle circular motion, rub the cardstock together as if you were pre-treating a laundry stain. Gradually, work your way around the cardstock until you get the desired effect.

Accents

Simple accents can be added to your pictures, borders, and backgrounds to create an air of softness and elegance. Simply rub chalk (or eye shadow) along the edges of the paper. The colour of chalk chosen can be either a similar colour to the background, a contrasting colour, or an outlining colour such as black or grey depending on the result you want.

Punching

Basically punching is the cutting out of an image or piece of text using a cookie cutter like tool. Most punches are made of die cast steel. They come in various shapes and sizes. Photographs and text blocks can be punched into virtually any shapes or sizes. These shapes can add to the impact of the themes. For instance, pictures of your sweetheart can be punched into heart shapes to add to the romantic type of love. Alternately, small doves can be punched and placed along the borders to add a romantic touch to a wedding scrapbook. Titles and text can also be punched to create professional looking scrapbook pages.

When punching out and gluing small pieces of paper, place a strip of double-sided tape on the paper before punching out the shape. Next, just punch the tape into shape. Then, the piece is immediately ready to place.

Coloured Paper

Additional colour can be easily added to the scrapbook page through different coloured backgrounds, borders, and embellishments. A light coloured background creates a soft, farther away feeling; while a darker background sharpens the focus. Complimentary colours can be slightly lighter or darker than the background to direct the focus towards or away from portions of the page. Contrasting colours can also be used to create a more dramatic or focusing effect away from or towards various photographs or mementos. Simply add, fold, or paste additional sheets of paper into your design for the desired effect.

Vellum

Vellum is a transparent, translucent material. Vellum can be used to create a slight shadow or shade change to background or embellishment colours. This can be used as a softening agent for baby scrapbooks, as a touch of elegance to gift scrapbooks, or to create dimension in a boring flat page. To reduce the cloudiness effect caused by gluing, apply only a thin line of glue along the edges of the vellum. In this way, you will see a slight shadow only along the very edge. This will look like a border to the vellum. Vellum is available in both acidic and non acidic forms.

Shadow Boxes

A great way to add depth to the scrapbook page is to add shadow boxes. Basically shadow boxes add a shadow to your images. Shadow boxes are also a great way to make your most important photographs or text boxes stand out form the rest of the page. Shadow boxes can also be to emphasis dedications.

To make a shadow box, simply cut a box shape out of paper. Next, put your embellishment on a larger square of cardstock. Then, add glue to all four sides of the cardstock square and attach it to the back of your paper. The embellishment will show through, adding greater dimension to your page.

Adding Dimension

One good way to add dimension to images is to use double stick foam tape. Double stick foam tape literally allows items to pop out at your reader adding realism to items. This technique is especially useful in children's art and educational scrapbooks.

Simply, cut the foam tape into whatever shape and size you want. Then, attach to shape onto your scrapbook page. Double stick foam tape is available at most craft stores in various colours and thicknesses.

Common Business Mistakes.

All entrepreneurs have to learn from their own mistakes as they build their business, but wouldn't it be great to have some one tell you what the common mistakes are and how to avoid them? You Want a Successful Business – So Do not Do This!

- **Believing that you will start earning straight away**. All businesses take time to establish themselves – even internet based ones. People need to know where you are, what you sell and most importantly, that they can trust your company to deliver what it promises. Expect to spend at least 6 months working away at your business before you break even – sometimes longer.
- **Believing that you can set up a business and it continually earns for you.** Even a very profitable business needs continual management to ensure that your profit does not erode. Your products and marketing need to continually change to meet the changing circumstances in the real world.
- **Believing in Get Rich Quick Schemes:** A good business is established by part inspiration, part perspiration and just a little bit of luck!
- **Believing that you can earn whilst you are aware from the office.** Even if you fully automate your business and hire really good staff, there is always an element of "while the

cat is away". That is why there are so many "absent owner" sales.

- **Being a single product company.** As good as your product may be, markets and tastes will change and so must you. If your product is very good – other companies will quickly take action to seize your market share by bringing in similar products at cheaper prices.
- **Not offering upgrades and enhancements.** It is far easier and cheaper to sell to existing customers. You do this by offering upgrades and enhancements to their existing products. You should have a group of products at several increasing price points.
- **Relaxing after you success.** Businesses need continual effort, management and improvements. Although a product launch is hard work, you should start on your next product shortly afterwards. This will give you sustainable success and several income streams.
- **Believing that a business can be established with little capital.** Marketing, infrastructure purchases, stock, advertising and staff all cost money and must be purchased in order to make a profit. Cash flow kills more business than anything else.
- **Not investing in your staff.** Your staff are the public face of your business. They should be well trained, knowledgeable and well dressed as well as fully motivated to sell on your behalf.

- **Not motivating** your staff. Good staff are hard to find and difficult to keep. They help your business expand and be profitable. They will grow your business exponentially as word of mouth spreads.
- **Believing that you know all you have to**. Your competitors may have been in the business longer than you have, your customers may be very knowledgeable. Meeting customer needs is a constantly changing landscape and you need to keep up to date on the latest trends and technology. You need to be able to project yourself as an expert in the field you work in. If you do not have this knowledge then learn it or buy it in!
- **Branding.** It is important that your company is recognised and has a good image. This helps spread the word about your services! Otherwise why would your customers hire you? Spend on your brand, it is worth it!

Learn these lessons well, avoid the mistakes at all costs you should save valuable time and resources by doing things right the first time.

Standing Out From The Crowd

You've heard about a Unique Selling Point and guess that you want one but you have no idea what it is and why you need one. Often called the U.S.P – it means – "What makes your company, product and services different from all the other companies selling the same thing? Now obviously in a crowded business environment – be it click or brick – you want your company to not only stand out but be memorable. You USP will do this for you.

So how do I define my USP?

Have a look at you company and a few companies that you believe compete with you. Also look at a couple of companies who are trading as you would wish to trade in the next few years. For products we mean products, goods or services.

So, what product features could you have that would make you different from your competitors?

- Look at what products you sell the most often or most of.
- How do these products differ from each other?
- What benefits do these products provide?
- What better features do you/ you could provide?
- What features do competitor's products have that yours do not?
- What features do your products have that are different you are your competitors?

Make yourself stand out from your competitors and emphasise this in all your fully branded marketing materials and you should not only stand out from others but also look larger, more professional and memorable.

Branding, The How's, What's And Why's

Your business brand says a lot about you and your business. If you create a strong brand image, it will elevate you above your peers and provide a good model for your product and service development as well as a sound foundation from which to expand your business.

What is Branding?

Many people think that having a logo and maybe a short description of their services is all they need to set up their brand. This is not so.

Your brand encompasses all that your business does, from first contact with your potential customers through to how your products are defined and sold. Your brand is what defines and describes your business. Look at any two different companies that compete in the same market and look at how people recognise and remember them.

For example look at Rolls Royce and Toyota - they both sell cars but each company is known for a different reason. Someone looking for a car on a budget would not go to Rolls Royce - yet both sell their cars on reliability.

Clearly more people would aspire to purchase a Rolls Royce, but many also be happy to purchase a Toyota.

Look again at the perceived value of a brand. Why is the iPod the desired MP3 product when other brands have similar properties and reliabilities? People perceive the ipod to be superior and are willing to pay more for the pleasure of owning one. Indeed many people would not consider any other purchase. This is clever branding by Apple who marketed their product as being very desirable to certain markets.

I Do not Have that Kind of Money - So Why do I Need to Create my Own Brand?

The main reason has to be to differentiate yourself. You are starting a business in a very crowded market so you need to stand out from the hobby workers and other competitors.

Branding also makes the promotion of your company and development of your products so much easier. There are thousands of new businesses and many times more web sites.

You need to:
- Set yourself apart from the competition
- Make yourself memorable so that people will either look for your business or choose you above your competitors.

- When introducing your business to a new customer, your brand should go before you and communicate much of what you want to say.

So How Do I Create My Own Brand Then?

You brand must say:
- Who you are.
- What you do.
- How you do it.
- What the benefits of using your business are.

You brand MUST establish your company and build your credibility with your prospective customers.

In order to be able to do this you must first be able to describe what you want your business and products say, so start with your Mission Statement or Elevator Statement.

- **The Mission Statement** - this is what you want your business to be or do as it operates. You need to be realistic and focused. Being profitable is not a mission statement, but deciding what you want to do to be profitable is.
- **The Elevator Statement** - This is 1-4 sentences that you would use to describe your business, in the time that it takes to travel in an elevator - or a few minutes. It is used when meeting new people who ask "and what do you do?" or as an introduction when networking.

Profitable New Scrapbooking Business

What Should Be Described Within My Brand?

First of all, pretend that you are one of your target customers and list 5 things that they will be seeking from your product. These items would encompass a short definition of one of more of the following:

- Price.
- Quality.
- Service.
- Support.
- Scarcity or availability.
- How and when delivered.
- Accessibility.
- Security.

So now define who, what and where you are in these terms and you should come up with something like this as a Mission Statement.

"We will provide quality wedding memory scrapbooks in Suburbia. Our quality scrapbooks will be part of the couple's memories of a happy day"

Your elevator pitch might be something like this: "We provide quality memory based wedding scrapbooks to happy couples in Suburbia."

Tag Line

Now need to be recognised by your customers. Here is where you tag line and logo comes into play.

My tag line - what's that.

Well if you become as well known as Nike it can be something very short like "Just Do It" - but that is a few years and few £million down the road. Your tag line is a short description of what you do.

Something like "Memories are captured in our wedding scrapbooks" which explains what you sell and to whom. It also differentiates you from other companies in your area.

Logo's

Now you need a logo - it does not need repeating that this should also reflect your brand. If you are saying you are modern and efficient - you do not want an old fashioned, messy looking logo. It should always reflect your brand and be simple and recognisable. You should include it on:

- All your communications.
- Your web site.
- Your products.
- Your packaging.
- Your marketing, adverts and promotional materials.

Working with your Brand

Your brand is so much more than your logo; it is your company name, your web site and the colours that you use.

Remember your brand allows you to pre-sell your company and products as well as ease the introduction of new products as you become more established. Be consistent with your brand promotion - do not keep changing it as people are more likely to remember things the more they see them. Regular marketing enables you to establish your credibility and relevance to your target market.

Branding, Packaging and other Stuff

Everything that your customers and staff see should be "stamped" with your company brand and be instantly recognised as belonging to your company. Let us look at where your will be using your brand. Invoices and order forms should have your company details, contact details and web site as well as your logo.

Business Name

Pick a great business name that reflects the type of scrapbooks you are selling and who you are selling to. If you are getting a domain name (and you should, even if you do not want a web site just yet) you need to match this with your company name. As relative domain names are quite hard to find, best to start searching for them first.

Packaging

It stands to reason that all your bags and packaging, including that used in delivering your items, should be stamped with your company name, logo, phone number and web site. All packaging should include further Order Forms, and a catalogue.

Marketing Material

Once again, when you market your company, it should be instantly recognisable from your logo and your branding. How and where you advertise should also back up your brand image. If you are selling family friendly items then you would not advertise in a "lad's mag" for example.

Your business cards should obviously have your logo and use your chosen colours and fonts. The design of your business cards and your brochure should be similar and follow the general ethos of your company branding. You can your marketing material designed by an independent designer or you can go to some very large design web sites such as vista or template web sites and obtain design ideas from them. They will usually professionally print them off and deliver them to you as well. Web sites such as cafépress will also provide you with other marketing materials such as mugs, caps, totes etc.

Starting Small With Your Premises

This is not the type of business that you can afford to start from a retail shop so why not think about starting a kart or kiosk in a shopping mall? Here are a few points to consider.

Mall Karts and Kiosks

As always Location, Location, Location: The location of your business is crucial to its survival. A store's location can often spell its success or failure. Without sufficient store recognition, a business can suffer poor cash flow and will inevitably fail over time. Your business needs to be physically located out in midst of everyday life, in broad daylight where shoppers can easily find you.

The location itself of the mall plays a huge role in your kart's success. Is the mall located in an isolated part of the city or town, or right in the heart of the action?

You must forecast the level as well as the timing of traffic your business will receive during the morning, midday, and late afternoon on each day of the week. Therefore, you can efficiently establish an employment schedule as well as appropriate operating hours.

Choose your mall carefully so that it has ample traffic of potential customers. Go there with a "clicker" and see how many people pass by per hour. Visit on several different days of the week as well as at different times.

Profitable New Scrapbooking Business

Quality of Traffic: It is one thing to have steady traffic, and another to have the kind of traffic that your business needs. Some malls attract low-to-middle income people; others are targeted towards the upper class. Choose wisely.

Position in the Mall: Your success in a mall will depend on whether you are located in a section that is conducive to what your business is selling. You should look at the **complementary nature of the adjacent stores.** Look for businesses that are complimentary to what you are selling such as craft or hobby shops. You may want to be located near a restaurant where people are already in their "hunger fulfilling" state of mind.

Similarly **high volume areas** where lines of patrons form, such as theatres or department stores, are also good mall locations as it could give potential customers several minutes to look in your display or listen to your sales pitch. People will hopefully spend while they wait – if not you have their undivided attention for some time and they will remember you.

Costs: Rental costs in shopping malls are often higher than rates in downtown Main Street. You main consideration should be: will the higher traffic compensate for the increased rental cost? If you can easily recover your monthly rental payment and overhead expenses, you are in a good position to make a profit.

Profitable New Scrapbooking Business

People Buy with their Eyes! Ensure that you display your products in a tempting manner. Karts, kiosks, stalls and vans and are very good in selling items that are "impulse buys". Make your products appealing and your sales pitch interesting and your sales will increase!

Market Stalls and Boot Fairs

The same criteria about location appertains to market stalls and boot fairs. Obviously your outlay will be much smaller – but so will your potential income. Care should be taken to ensure that your stall looks professional and well branded otherwise your business will be classed as a "hobby business" and people will expect to pay correspondingly low prices.

Marketing From Your Retail Site

Whichever low cost option you chose, ensure that you have plenty of brochures available to give out to interested potential customers. Do not leave them on the counter otherwise you will go through a lot of them for little return – save them for the really interested people. You could leave business cards for anyone to take- people tend to take these only if they are interested. You should display some good samples as well as a lot of items for sale. Be prepared to take orders from your stall.

Marketing Your Business

The first thing you need to do is contact your friends and neighbours and see if they need your services or know someone who does. This usually gets you a few sales to start with. You can consider selling at "mates rates" – discounted rates in order to get yourself some experience and references.

Now set up an advert on your PC. You can print them off, on postcards quite easily, or you can visit your local design site that will do this for you. It should read something like this.

Build your memories with our beautifully designed Scrapbooks

For more details,

Call: 123-4567 - ABC Scrapbooks

www.ABCScrapbooks.com

If you do not feel that you can do this yourself. Then go to Vistaprint, Lulu etc. who will print some off for you at not too high a price. You can also put a similar advert in your local papers if that is affordable.

In essence, you now have a professional advertising "billboard" and it is time to use a bit of shoe leather. Put the leaflets on notice boards in supermarkets, shops, clubs, offices etc. Always ask first.

Profitable New Scrapbooking Business

If you want to sell to clubs, societies, hotels etc then now is the time to "dial and smile". You need to get contact details from the yellow pages, internet or your contacts. Call them up or send them your information pack, with the aim of obtaining an appointment to discuss your services. The next chapter explains what to do on this appointment.

If you also decided to use business cards – use the front to put your company name, contact details and a one line description of your services. Start to leave these wherever you are allowed to - anywhere busy people and new parents or pet owners can be found.

A good supply of business cards for your staff as well, in order to advertise your services to others they come in contact with.

A great idea would be to have magnetic signs made for your company and services. Place these signs on the sides of the cars your people use for transportation to each job, and later on, to the sides of your company van or car.

One other form of advertising you should go with would be a display ad in the yellow pages of your telephone directory.

Look at getting yourself a stall at the local market, the car boot sale, a kiosk in the mall etc. which will get you a lot of exposure and hopefully some sales for little outlay. We go into this later in the book.

Profitable New Scrapbooking Business

Home parties are one of the best and most economical ways to market the scrapbooking products. Tupperware ladies and Avon consultants have been selling this way for years. Ask friends and family to host parties for you. Distribute your catalogues and be sure your phone number and e-mail address are featured prominently. We will talk about this concept later in this book.

See if your community college offers scrapbooking courses and see if the instructor will distribute some of your business cards to those taking the class. They will usually be happy to do so unless the college prohibits it.

You can also sponsor workshops where people get together to work on their scrapbooks. This is a prime opportunity to strike while the passion is hot. People may look at your book and love what you did with the page about your family vacation. That is a perfect time to whip out your catalogue and show them the papers or die cuts that you used from your company. We will also look at seminars and workshops later in this book.

Other Marketing Tools

There are a lot of other ways to promote your business. You may want to look into give-away items that you can offer as free gifts during crops or workshops. If you decide to do a trade show, these gifts will be immensely popular!

Profitable New Scrapbooking Business

Many people go the traditional key chain/pen route with your business name on it. This is great, but you are a scrapbooking business. Why not make your giveaways a little more pertinent to the scrapbooking venue?

Craft bags can be an excellent marketing tool. These can be simple carry-alls with your company information screen printed on the front. Give them away at crops and/or workshops so people can carry their materials in them. This is advertising that is out there all the time and can generate interest in your company just by having people carry them around.

You can have pens imprinted with your company name and information, but instead of the standard ink pen, why not choose a decorative type of pen like a glitter ink or coloured marker that your customer can actually use when they are scrapbooking?

There are many other items that you can look at such as customized sticker pages, mini albums with your name on the back cover, specialty scissors, rubber stamps, etc. These products are out there, just seek them out and spend a little extra money by adding them to your marketing arsenal!

Tips to Overcoming Stage Fright

The first thing you need to understand about stage fright is that it is not uncommon at all. Some of the greatest actors, politicians and other public figures known to society experience the phenomenon every time they get in front of an audience. In short, stage fright is a perfectly rational and human response to a social situation.

For most people, that initial level of anxiety quickly subsides once on stage and into the business at hand. However, if you find that your stage fright tends to linger, there are a few different tricks you can employ in order to help things along and focus on the business at hand.

First, remind yourself people do not die of stage fright. Second, when is the last time you personally knew someone fainting from stage fright? Chances are you do not, in spite of what you see in the movies or have heard about from vague sources.

The truth is that the anxiety of stage fright is simply a little extra adrenalin coursing through your system. Your body is a wonderful device that knows how to shut down the adrenalin flow before there is too much. So realize that if you do not feed the anxiety by thinking it will never end, your initial bout will be over in just a few minutes.

Profitable New Scrapbooking Business

Second, forget about making a fool of yourself in front of other people. This is the foundation for most cases of stage fright. Remind yourself that you are prepared and you are a professional. You know how to do this right. Because you are in control, you will not embarrass yourself. Instead, people are expecting to learn something and will inn fact be very happy to be in your presence for the course of your time on stage.

Last, pick out a few people around the audience to address. While your remarks are intended for everyone present, identifying a few faces that seem to be especially welcoming will help to trick your brain into thinking in terms of having a conversation with just a handful of people – a much less anxious situation for most people.

As you calm down and get into the swing of your presentation, you will quickly find you are having that private conversation with more and more people.

One final word of advice – do not dread stage fright. It is a useful tool that will help you to stay mentally alert and on top of things. That is why many stage actors get really nervous if they do not experience stage fright before stepping onto the stage for the first time that night – they just know their relaxed attitude is going to lead to dropping a line or missing a cue.

So see your initial stage fright as your mind's way of getting you ready to give the best presentation ever!

Giving A Compelling Presentation

Here are a few ways to make that scrapbooking presentation compelling and intriguing to your attendees.

Make **use of visual aids.** Use a large screen to project slides, images, and animation as a backdrop for your remarks. The combination of visual and audio stimulation will help your presentation to connect with just about everyone in the audience.

Be animated yourself. No, you do not have to constantly be in motion. Actually, that might be distracting and possibly even irritating. But let your facial expressions and the tone of your voice convey interest and excitement about the subject matter. People will respond in kind.

Arrange the presentation so people have a chance to absorb what you are saying. A good rule of thumb is no more than twenty minutes of feeding them information before changing the programme a little. The change can be something as simple as stopping for questions, giving everybody a minute to stretch, or breaking the audience into small groups to do some brainstorming. The variety will help to keep the presentation fresh and alive.

Keep the mood casual. When people are relaxed, they tend to listen. Often, they will get so involved in the presentation that the time will fly by. Count this as a good thing, since it means you are doing a great job.

Being a successful presenter means knowing how to hold the attention of your audience, and when to give them a break from listening to you. Make use of positive body language and tones, and make sure your subject matter is informative and presented with some variety. When you include all these elements, you will find the presentation to be a huge success.

10 Tips for Professional Speakers

Put your best foot forward every time! One of the reasons that many people fear taking the podium is because they are afraid of being the focal point of everyone's attention and they do not want to make a fool of themselves. There are several things you can do to "fool-proof" your speaking event so that you present well every single time!

1. **Take the time to prepare well for your presentation.** Preparation enhances your confidence and it is also an opportunity to refine any weak areas in your presentation.

2. **Begin and end your presentation on time.** Arriving late to your presentation is simply unprofessional; not to mention that it won't win you any points with your crowd.

3. **Know your audience.** The only way you can really relate your audience is if you know who they are. Profile your audience. Are they male or female? What income bracket are they in? Why would they attend your presentation?

4. **Dress appropriately for your audience.** Not all speaking engagements require a business suit! There are many places where business casual attire has become the norm. Before your audience even hears your message, they are already sizing you up and this is impacting whether or not they are hearing what you have to say!

5. **Have a backup plan for visual aids** used in your presentation. You have selected to use visual aids because you thought they would be helpful in getting your message across. What happens when laptops fail or the room cannot accommodate presentation equipment? Create a plan on how you would handle a situation like that.

6. **Tone down information overload.** Yes, you can overload your audience with too much information and if you are not careful, you'll lose them. They will mentally check out. As a speaker, you'll want to present enough information that hooks them into getting more information from you!

7. **Do not use inappropriate humour.** Humour can be a tricky thing working for you or against you. You will really have to know your audience in order to use jokes or humour appropriately.

8. **Vary your speech tones.** The monotonous speaker will lose their audience within the first 15 minutes. It is okay to be animated during your presentation and in fact, doing so will transmit flair and passion that keeps people engaged in your message.

9. **Relate your topic back to your audience.** Basically, stop talking about yourself! Your audience might want to hear a testimony or two, but mostly, they will want to hear about them and how your presentation can help them!

10. **Solidify your message.** Support your ideas with data and evidence and build a solid case for your viewpoints. You can use statistics, testimonies, demonstrations, pictures and more!

Your presentation can be fool proof if you take the time to minimise mistakes. By going through these key points, you can assure yourself that you are well prepared for any challenge that might come your way and you will experience the success you have always dreamed of!

Seminars

Seminars are a great way of earning money and a great skill to learn. You can either hold seminars to promote your own business or as part of your consultancy or training offering.

Setting Up Your Seminar

In any seminar, there are basic pieces of information that an audience should receive from their presenter. You are the problem solver presenting a solution that will benefit your audience. The presentation should answer who, what, when, where, why and how regarding your topic. In giving that information, your presentation will have clarity and will be on track to give the detail necessary to your audience.

Who - Who is your target audience? What would they like to know about regarding your presentation? Do they have any preconceived notions about your material? What are their concerns?

Are you addressing the "who" you targeted in your research? When you address the "who" of your message, you are better able to relate with your audience. They will feel like you are speaking directly to them. They will give you their attention because they feel like their needs are being addressed.

What - What is the message you want to communicate? What are the issues? What are the solutions? The "what" in your message is the backbone of your presentation. It is your purpose of your message and the reason you are speaking. It is also the reason why people come to hear you.

When - When is the recommended time to take action? Is there a sense of urgency in your presentation? Stressing the "when" aspect of your message is especially important when you want your audience to take action immediately following the presentation - i.e. - sign up for a class, sell promotional materials, implement what was learned)

Where - Where is the problem located? Where can your audience find the help they need? "Where" signifies direction. This leads your audience somewhere in your presentation. Where would you like to take them? Common "where" statements include "across America today", "in college campuses nationwide", and "in families in California".

Why - Why should they take action? What are the motivating factors in prompting your audience to take action? The main focus here is inspiration and motivation to take action. Not only do you want them to listen to you, but you want your audience to take action on what you've said. You want to somehow improve their lives and honing your message on the "why" is a critical necessity.

How - How can they respond to your message? How can they take action based on what they've heard? This is the learning and teaching portion of your message. This can be the "how-to" section telling them how they can easily improve their lives. This section often incorporates steps to follow.

As you piece all of these bits of information together, you'll be giving your audience the detailed answers they are looking for. You also present yourself as the credible source of information you want to present yourself to be!

Organising Your Seminar

One of the most difficult aspects of making your presentation is getting started. You may be feeling overwhelmed even if you have been working with your materials for years but the first step is to jump in there and get started.

Research your material. Collect and read as much information as possible. Make some notes and also look at the validity of the information you are collecting. Is the information outdated? Is it relevant to the actual subject you are going to talk about? Start taking notes and highlighting potentially key points of your presentation.

Profitable New Scrapbooking Business

Review. Once you feel you've gathered enough information to present, review your notes and select the information you are going to present. Look for key ideas that support the purpose of your talk. Decide how deep you will go when presenting your information? Consider your audience. What do they need to know to take action on your subject? How much detail do they actually need? Consider also, the length of the time you'll have for your presentation.

Organize your key ideas into an outline form. Start with the key points you will make and add two to three supporting elements to it. When you speak, you will be leading your audience from point A to point B. You are taking them somewhere even if it's only in their minds. Does your outline show a path to take? Is it relevant? Adjust your key points until you do lead your audience to where you want them to go.

Decide how you will present your organised information in your presentation. What visual aids can you use to strengthen your points? Is there data or research that you can bring into your presentation? How can you vary the delivery of your message? Your presentation will be more interesting if you do more than just talk. People can easily tune out of your message especially if it is during a meal or immediately following.

Organize your presentation outline to incorporate your visuals and method of delivery in your presentation. Review what it looks like on paper. Your outline is like your map for success. Is your map clearly defining the information you want to say? Are there any weak points were the information is not as strong as you'd like it to be? If it's not, revise and review and keep doing this until you get your map the way you want it to be.

Organising the material for your presentation is a process. As you take your audience from lack of knowledge to having knowledge, create a seminar outline map of the journey. This map is the key to your success and the only way to be successful is to have a plan of action.

Charisma Matters!

If you want to take your scrapbooking expertise on the road, then offering seminars may be just the ticket. Of course, you will need to do more than just present a dry recitation of facts and figures. Like any type of public figure who takes center stage for an event, you have to be able to hold the attention of your audience. In short, you need to have a good dose of charisma.

Charisma means different things to different people. But at the end of the day, it is the result of your charisma that you want to focus on.

Profitable New Scrapbooking Business

You want people to listen to you. You want people to trust you. You want people to respect you enough to put your suggestions into action. Basically, you want people to like you.

Cultivating your coaching persona can mean taking on several attributes. It is a good idea to make sure those attributes come naturally to you. Otherwise you come off as artificial and stilted at best, or just plain phony at worst. Here are some attributes that are likely to help you hold the attention of the audience.

Humor. No, you do not have to dress like a clown or constantly tell jokes in order to be humorous – unless that is relevant to the seminar! But humor has a way of helping people to relax and enjoy what is going on around them. A little humor scattered through your presentation will help people to settle in and be comfortable enough to absorb all that wonderful education you are providing.

Verbiage. While technical terms may be necessary up to a point, you also want to keep your presentation accessible to a wide audience. To some extent, you want the presentation to be more like a conversation between friends, and less like a lecture in a college classroom. Using this approach helps people settle down and digest what you are saying in easy bites that go down very easy.

Accessibility. If at all possible, make sure there are ways for people to ask questions or make comments. Vary this a little by providing both time for people to verbally pose a question or offer a comment, and also some means of doing so in a private manner. For example, you can provide pads and pencils that people can write down questions. Instruct them to fold the paper in half and drop them into a receptable when leaving the conference room for a break. Nobody has to know who asked the question in this manner.

All these qualities will translate well into conducting seminars via a web conference. Thus, you really do not have to change your basic style when moving from one medium to another. This helps you be the same person all the time, which is less of a strain on maintaining your persona, and also helps people to see you as being real no matter what the setting happens to be.

Tips to Overcoming Stage Fright

The first thing you need to understand about stage fright is that it is not uncommon at all. Some of the greatest actors, politicians and other public figures known to society experience the phenomenon every time they get in front of an audience. In short, stage fright is a perfectly rational and human response to a social situation.

Profitable New Scrapbooking Business

For most people, that initial level of anxiety quickly subsides once on stage and into the business at hand. However, if you find that your stage fright tends to linger, there are a few different tricks you can employ in order to help things along and focus on the business at hand.

First, remind yourself people do not die of stage fright. When is the last time you personally knew someone fainting from stage fright? Chances are you do not, in spite of what you see in the movies or have heard about from vague sources.

The truth is that the anxiety of stage fright is simply a little extra adrenalin coursing through your system. Your body is a wonderful device that knows how to shut down the adrenalin flow before there is too much. So realize that if you do not feed the anxiety by thinking it will never end, your initial bout will be over in just a few minutes.

Second, forget about making a fool of yourself in front of other people. This is the foundation for most cases of stage fright. Remind yourself that you are prepared and you are a professional.

You know how to do this right. Because you are in control, you will not embarrass yourself. Instead, people are expecting to learn something and will inn fact be very happy to be in your presence for the course of your time on stage.

Lastly, pick out a few people around the audience to address. While your remarks are intended for everyone present, identifying a few faces that seem to be especially welcoming will help to trick your brain into thinking in terms of having a conversation with just a handful of people – a much less anxious situation for most people.

As you calm down and get into the swing of your presentation, you will quickly find you are having that private conversation with more and more people.

One final word of advice – do not dread stage fright. It is a useful tool that will help you to stay mentally alert and on top of things.

That is why many stage actors get really nervous if they do not experience stage fright before stepping onto the stage for the first time that night – they just know their relaxed attitude is going to lead to dropping a line or missing a cue.

So see your initial stage fright as your mind's way of getting you ready to give the best presentation ever!

Back of the Room Sales?

Back of the Room Sales are material that are sold in the back of the room, before during or after your seminar. Many audiences like to take information home with them, and Back of the Room products give them this opportunity. What kinds of items make good Back of the Room Sales?

Here is a starter list:
- Books.
- CD/DVD sets.
- Study courses.
- Promotional items.
- Other services, such as coaching.

Books. This is the most obvious. There is no quicker way to enhance your credibility that to write and publish a book. In some big-city markets, such as Los Angeles, it is difficult if not impossible to secure a speaking engagement without having published a book. But do not let the word publish scare you. Yes, it is lovely if you can get an established New York publisher to bring out your book. However, it is not the only path. It is legitimate to write and publish your own book, and it doesn't even have to be that long. Look into Print on Demand companies. These firms publish books as people order them, one at a time. This is ideal for your website, but can also work for Back of the Room Sales. Simply order several yourself and have them available to look at and if you run out, hand out cards with easy ordering information. Many experts recommend getting a book out as soon as possible, so start writing now!

CD/DVD sets. This can be a videotape of your speech, or a longer DVD of your workshops. If you are presenting a keynote seminar, for instance, many people may be interested in your longer presentations and thus buy a DVD of your workshop to take home and watch at their leisure.

Profitable New Scrapbooking Business

You can also put some of your training courses onto CD or if you are really organised onto a DVD.

DVD's are very easy to produce now. Get yourself a cheap video camera – like the flip or Kodak series and a small stand. Set the camera up whilst you are preparing a piecing or scrapbook and record what you do, giving instructions as you progress as if you were telling someone in front of you what to do. Pretend you are on Blue Peter or Sesame Street if it helps!

Study Courses. As the name implies, a study course is a longer and multi-part publication. It can be on CDs or published style. Often the best study courses are a combination—CD of the material accompanied by a workbook.

Promotional Items. Many speakers like to sell or give away pens or pencils or notebooks emblazoned with a catch-phrase or funny quip. Look for items that tie into your presentation. Some speakers develop a collection of small toys or accessories that they sell. Computer consultants may sell mouse pads or other accessories.

Other services. One of the most lucrative Back of the Room products can be selling services such as coaching or mentoring sessions.

Profitable New Scrapbooking Business

Once audiences have been won over by your wonderful presentations, they are often hungry for more. Many of them would like to work with you and so it will be to your benefit to develop extra services that you can offer.

All of these Back of the Room products are excellent additions to your seminar income. They may not bring in a lot of money, but they are good ways to keep your name in front of people and add credibility. Over time, Back of the Room products can provide you with a nice additional income stream.

Party Selling

Every party should be planned, and follow a prescribed format or agenda. This is because without a plan, it will just be a gathering of people wasting time at your home instead of theirs. You must have a plan to know what to do next in order to achieve the desired results. Having a "pattern" is also the easiest way to teach others to duplicate your success, and the idea of following a successful formula is a proven method of making the most sales in the least time.

Phase one is the greeting and get-acquainted time slot - about thirty minutes. The hostess greets the guests as they arrive, prints a name tag for each, introduces them around, gives them a catalogue, points out the refreshments, and leads them into conversation with the other guests.

The second phase is the "game-playing" portion of your part. This phase is used to relax everybody and get them involved in the party. It should last about 15 to 20 minutes.

Presentation phase is the merchandise presentation by the host, who shows and describes each item on display. Ask different guests to inspect particular items and show the others what these articles look like in use.

Profitable New Scrapbooking Business

The length of time spent on this phase of the party will depend in large part on how much merchandise you have on display, but generally, you shouldn't spend more than about 20 minutes showing and describing your merchandise.

Then give your guests about 10 to 15 minutes to personally inspect and try on/inspect the items that have aroused their interest.

Administration

Be sure you have name tags for your guests, and a couple of felt tip marking pens. And do not forget the order forms. These should be standard two-piece self-carbon order forms - one copy for your customer and the other for your files. The best idea is to have printed your own order forms with your logo, contact details and sales message printed on them.

Another item to remember is your merchandise catalogues. Be sure you have a good supply on hand, all printed with your logo and address.

You could purchase these items and stamp your own details on them – but this does not instil anywhere near as much confidence in your company.

Your First Party

To get your start in this fabulous method of merchandising, become a host or host yourself. Give a few parties yourself, and learn the ropes.

Choose an evening for your party - any evening excepting Friday through the weekend. Generally 7:30 is the most convenient time for the greatest number of people. If it is inconvenient for whatever reason to hold a party in your home, arrange with a friend to hold the first couple of parties.

Make up a list of 30 to 60 people you can invite to the party. They can be friends, neighbours, relatives or people you know from work, even acquaintances with whom you do business such as the check-out clerk where you buy your groceries or people you meet at the bus stop on your way to work.

After formally inviting these people, you then call to remind them of the party at least a couple of days before the date of the party. This is important, because of the original 40 people you invite, at least 15 will not show because it slipped their minds, last minute circumstances that force a change in plans, and those that really weren't interested in the first place.

Profitable New Scrapbooking Business

On the day of the party, get your merchandise display set up early. The party should be held in the largest room in the home - usually the living room - with the merchandise display the centre of attraction.

The merchandise should be set out on a sturdy table covered with a good white or light coloured cloth, and the merchandise should be arranged by group or type.

Try to put a bit of imagination and showmanship into your merchandise display. This will have the effect of making your merchandise look much more valuable than it actually is. Those that do put flair into their merchandise displays find that it in creases their sales by as much as 25 percent over an ordinary showing.

Besides your merchandise display, be sure also you are organised with your refreshments. These usually consist of coffee, tea, soft drinks, cookies or other "nibble" items. The host or host usually makes arrangements in advance for one of the guests to assist with the serving of refreshments.

About a half hour before your guests are due to begin arriving, turn on all the lights in the room where the party is to be held. This will give the room a bright, warm feeling conducive to a party kind of atmosphere. And by all means, be sure to turn off all the radios, stereo and TV sets. Eliminate any and all noises from other rooms in your home that might distract the attention of your guests.

Profitable New Scrapbooking Business

You should mingle and converse with the guests during this time period in order to answer specific questions or explain the possible uses of an item, where it might look good in the buyer's home, and any interesting tid bits relating to where an item came from, how it was made, or the satisfaction of an earlier buyer.

When you seem to have answered all the questions and everyone appears to have made their selections, start writing orders. Do not hesitate to ask for orders. Writing orders should take about 15 minutes, and then you should let the party begin to winding down.

When you give a gift to the host for having the party, the presentation should be a special ceremony staged with all the "Show Biz" flair you can muster, at the end of your merchandise showing. However, when your gift is a cash award, carry your presentation over to the next party and make a big production of it as well. Do not forget to invite the "guest of honour" to your next scheduled party for the big presentation.

During these presentations many of the other guests will be favourably impressed, and as a consequence will ask you for details of becoming a host themselves.

During this time, mingle with your guests and anyone showing a spark of interest should be approached with an offer to serve as a future host or host.

Profitable New Scrapbooking Business

As each guest starts to leave, thank them for coming and walk with them to the door.

The total length of your party shouldn't be much more than two hours. Time and time again, it is been proven that you can do everything necessary, and make the most sales in this period of time. You lose effectiveness and make fewer sales with appreciably more or less time.

Recruiting New Hosts

There are a couple of proven ways to recruit new hosts or hostesses from the people attending your party. First of all, watch the guests as they look over the merchandise, examine, admire and wish for something they do not quite have enough extra money to buy. When you have determined that a particular guest wants a specific item but can't quite fit it into the budget, simply take her aside to a secluded corner of the room, and explain privately that you are willing to give her the item they has been looking at and wanting, if they will agree to invite her friends and relatives to a party in her home.

This approach works almost every time, and your only expense is the wholesale price of the item you give her as the free gift.

The second sure-fire approach is to offer a cash incentive. You do this by offering to allow 5% to 10% of the total sales volume resulting from the party staged for you by this type of new recruit.

Profitable New Scrapbooking Business

There is a plus factor for you on this one, because you'll be getting the enthusiastic participation of the host or host on the selling side. Once you have explained to them how your programme works, they will generally do everything they can to make the party a huge success, and thereby increase their pay for the evening.

Actually, your recruiting efforts should begin when you start taking orders. Every person you talk with should be offered the opportunity to hold a party of his or her own. Then just before the party begins breaking up, ask your guests as a group if any of them would be interested in holding a similar party in his or her home. You ask those who voice an interest to stay over for a few minutes in order to work out the details.

You should have an Appointment Book for this scheduling. Simply ask what date would be favourable for them, mark that date in the book, along with the name, address and telephone number. Then assure each that you'll call in the next day or two to work out the details.

Advertising

Many party plan merchandisers use a letter. They write a letter extolling the fun and excitement of the parties, explaining briefly the opportunities to receive free gifts of their choice or big commission checks. Then they invite the letter recipients to call for complete details on how they can stage a party.

These letters are usually printed in volume, and then slipped inside the covers of the catalogue these merchandisers give to each person attending the parties. Sometimes these letters are handed to each guest as the party breaks up.

Some party plan merchandisers also run small classified ads in the area newspapers. Their advertising plays up the opportunities available to make regular commission checks (extra income) simply by holding parties in their homes. People interested are invited to phone for more details. Response to this kind of ad is generally very good, with the conversion rate better than sixty percent!

Secrets of Success

Probably one of the greatest secrets of success with this kind of sales operation is that in order to make the sales, and talk about $400 parties, you must have the widest selection of merchandise possible.

Many beginners, not understanding that offering the potential buyers a wide and varied selection of items to choose from is what builds your profits in a hurry, base their entire merchandising plan around a selection that is of special interest or particularly appealing to themselves. It is all right to include the items that you especially like, but do not base your entire merchandise line on the things you like; you are selling to others, not yourself!

Profitable New Scrapbooking Business

Most successful party plan merchandisers advise that you should display at least forty different items and more if you have the supplier contacts or the buying expertise.

Still another important point to consider before buying merchandise to display and sell. Do the prices you have to pay for your products wholesale allow you enough room for a reasonable profit when compared to your time and expense?

Do some market research relative to your ambitions and when you are satisfied that you understand the workings of Party Plan Merchandising, grab the opportunity and run with it!

Trade Shows And Conventions

Almost every business in the world holds some type of trade show or convention whether it be nationally or locally. While some of these may seem out of the realm of possibility financially, you really can benefit greatly by attending these shows.

By going to a trade show or convention, you can make some amazing contacts that will grow your business. Networking is essential, and you can make some great new contacts at these events.

You can also get some great new ideas from the other scrapbookers who are attending the convention. Almost everyone will bring along their own books to show off what they can do. The purpose of conventions is to gain new insights into the business and learn from others, so take advantage of it! You can bet your fellow attendees will do the same!

Trade shows are a bit different. At trade shows, companies will set up booths showcasing their new products hoping to get some business from you in the future. This can be an excellent learning opportunity for you plus you get the advantage of meeting the people behind your supplies.

They will most likely be offering up discounts and perks as well in an attempt to get your business.

Profitable New Scrapbooking Business

Do not pass up any opportunity. Take their promotional items, get catalogues, make contacts, and use their services when you get home.

Often if you mention you saw them at a trade show, they'll be willing to offer you even more discounts with a bulk order. This can be a great way to procure even more supplies for your business at a discounted rate.

When you attend trade shows, there will probably be workshops and classes that you can attend that will showcase new techniques as well as hot items in the business. When you learn how to use these techniques, you can bring that skill back to your own business and have an edge over your competition.

Attend as many workshops as you can – they'll be well worth your time! They are included in the admission price of the trade show, so you may as well learn as much as you can while you are there.

Interacting With Your Customers

Once you spread the word that you are in the business of scrapbooking you will start to be busy and you need to be prepared to deal with your customers.

When prospective clients call or email you, explain your services and prices. When selling large or bespoke orders it is best to either ask for a 50% deposit or a 100% payment. This is because once you have finished the service; it is sometimes hard to obtain the payment due. Make sure that you receive all the payment due before you finish the service.

Scrapbooking Consultancy Services

When a prospective customer calls or your telephone sales pitch is positive, have your appointment book and a pen handy. Be friendly and enthusiastic. Explain what you do and offer to show a few samples.

When they ask how much you charge, simply give them a wide range and say that you will give a firm cost quote, once you have discussed their requirements. Then without much of a pause, ask if 4:30 this afternoon would be convenient for them, or if 5:30 would be better.

You must pointedly ask if they can come to make your cost proposal at a certain time, or the decision may be put off, and you may come up with a "no sale." You may prefer to invite them to visit you if you have a suitable reception area.

Just as soon as you have an agreement on the time and place to make you cost proposal and marked it in your appointment book, ask for their name, address and telephone number.

Jot this information down on a 3 by 5 card, along with the date and the notation: Prospective Customer. Then you file this card in a permanent card file.

Save these cards, because there are literally hundreds of ways to turn this prospect file into real cash, once you have accumulated a sizeable number of names, addresses and phone numbers. If you have a suitable computer programme, then enter the details there as well.

Estimating

When you go to see your prospect in person, always be on time. A couple of minutes early will not hurt you, but a few minutes late will definitely be detrimental to your closing the sale. If they are coming to you then ensure that you give good directions and are ready for them.

Profitable New Scrapbooking Business

Always be well groomed. Dress as a successful business owner. Be confident and sure of yourself; be knowledgeable about what you can do as well as understanding of the prospect's needs and wants. Do not smoke, even if invited by the prospect. It is important to appear methodical, thorough and professional. You need to create a good impression, and preserve it, by maintaining a business-like relation ship.

When you go to make your cost estimate, take along a ruled tablet on a clipboard a calculator, your appointment book and your sample designs.

You should also have at least two of your sales packs (one for the customer and the other for their friend that may also need your services) and a blank contract (more of this later). A receipt book would also be a good idea. You can buy folios in stationary stores that will keep these all tidy.

If they choose one of your sample designs, fine, but if they want a particular design of their own, now is the time to ask for photos or start jotting down all their requirements, including sizes and colours.

You should hopefully come up with a drawing or list of what they require in front of them. Get them to sign off these details and picture so that there is no dispute later. You will probably have to come back to them with a firm price. Make sure that it is possible for you to actually produce the scrapbook!

Profitable New Scrapbooking Business

Discuss when they need the scrapbook and if you are delivering or if they are collecting from you.

Now complete the contract for them, summarising what you have just agreed and confirm that you will send her a typed up list of all the scrapbook details you have just completed. Ask them for confirmation on the contract and for a deposit if applicable. Also offer them a sales pack for their friend who may need your services. Congratulations you have just made your first sale.

Seminars, Workshops and Training Courses

If you are running a seminar, workshop or training course, you will receive telephone calls and email enquiries. You should log all of these and ensure that you do not overbook your seminars etc. One way of doing this is by having a large wall planner or diary and writing down all confirmed the confirmed attendees against the relevant date. Those that are just enquiring but look definite can be written in pencil or other removable format.

You should request a deposit from all attendees to confirm their place and then full payment just before the course. This helps to provide definite numbers and saves you unnecessary expenses if they do not turn up. The deposit should be non refundable except in extenuating circumstances. It might be helpful to produce a standard letter or email to send people, noting all these details. You should also get together a brochure that you can send off to those enquiring about the course etc.

The Art of Selling

It has been said that a sale is really closed long before the seller makes the final pitch to the customer. In many ways, this is very true. Many customers make a decision to buy in five minutes or less of being introduced to the product. As a successful entrepreneur, it is up to you to make those five minutes really count.

There are a couple of important things that take place in this five minute window of opportunity.

First, the customer decides whether or not it is worth the time to learn more about the product. If the answer is no, then even thirty minutes of a great pitch will accomplish nothing.

Second, the customer will think of major obstacles that will prevent the purchase from taking place. If a customer decides the product is out of reach for some reason, that will make everything that follows that first five minutes of no value whatsoever.

Your job is to overcome both these issues and encourage the prospect to not only desire the product, but also be able to visualise actively using the product to great advantage.

Here are a few ideas on how to accomplish this:

- **Ascertain the needs of your client.** This means asking clarifying questions that help to narrow the focus of the presentation to what is important to the customer. For example, if a primary need of the client is to pay the phone bill at the end of the month, tailor the presentation to show how the product can directly help achieve that goal.
- **Be prepared to address common obstacles.** Many obstacles are not unique – people from all sorts of background will share the same concerns. Proactively bring those up during those first five minutes and quickly demonstrate how they are non-issues. This will make it possible to dispose of those concerns and hold the attention and interest of the prospect past that five minute window.
- **Always close with benefits**. Some of those benefits may have to do with overcoming obstacles, but go a little further than that. Using the phone bill example again, point out how the product can make it easier every month to pay the bill – not just the one that is due the end of this month.

Making the most of those first five minutes will greatly increase your chances of closing the sale. Spend some time working on a model presentation and critique the results. This will help you move with greater prowess when the real deal comes along. Congratulations you have just made a sale!

Administration

Administration is very important. Without good administration your company will quickly disintegrate into chaos and you will not know who has what and who needs to pay for services and who needs them to be cleaned and when.

Your administration should include ways of controlling or managing the following:
- Collecting money from your customers
- Banking money.
- Managing enquiries and complaints.
- Invoice and bill payment.
- Accounts and book keeping including, payroll, banking, taxes and VAT/taxes.
- Purchasing and auditing stock. At least once a year and preferably quarterly, stock must be checked against your accounts so that you know nothing is missing. On a more regular basis you should check to see if you need more stock.
- Salary and commission payments.
- Staff training and development.

It may seem a lot, but if you start small and get yourself a good accounts package, a good accountant and bank manager it is a lot easier.

Profitable New Scrapbooking Business

Customer Administration

- Set up a file for each of your customers with their contact details, what you have agreed to do, the price to be charged and any other details. Keep a folder/file for each customer. Add each order to the file – latest order on top. The file should include all contact details. If you have a number of orders per client put a list of orders on top and tick them off as you complete them. If you have a lot of customers have a customer number format.
- You should also keep a record of money due and paid. You should be able to find a good accounting system very easily. Always give a receipt and chase overdue accounts.
- Make a To-Do list of all your orders and tick off those that have been completed. Put in order of importance/when delivered. I had a wonderful system of putting a rail on the office wall and then collecting together each order with a clip. The clip then was hung on the rail so that it was easily seen. When the order was finished it came off the rail and was filed. In this way, I had a constant reminder of work to be done and it was easily found. Other people use wall planners or in trays – just find a system that works for you.
- Keep a detailed diary of when they have to be delivered by. In the diary also note what extra services were requested and what payment you need for the service.

Writing A Winning Proposal?

You've been working with a potential client and you think that you finally have the future project all worked out – then they ask you for a proposal. You have seen this great potential project but you need to bid for it. So how do you write that proposal that is going to win you the business?

Well first of all let's look at what the proposal should do. Win of course, but before that you have to:
- Make your company stand out from the others as well as reflect the values and brand of your company.
- Offer the solution that is required in a format that is easily understood.
- Be well priced so as to attract the client, provide a profit for your company as well as opportunities for you both to work together in the future.
- Be well structured, well written and well presented.

Bearing in mind the above, your proposal should look something like this:
1) Thanks for the opportunity.
2) Your understanding of the job that needs to be done.
3) How you would complete the job, how long it will take and who will do it.
4) Why your company is the best for the job.

5) Your price – with subject breakdowns if appropriate.

6) Any "must haves" assumptions made etc in getting to the price.

7) Last thanks and way forward.

Item 5 and 6 should be on their own page so that they can be removed if necessary.

Remember to put your company details and contact details on the header of each page and your copyrights, date and page number of number of pages on each footer.

When you send off the proposal, on time of course, include a brief cover letter, with:
- Your contact details.
- The name of the person who is their contact for this bid.
- Your thanks for the opportunity.
- A very brief overview of bid - no price.
- A time frame that bid is current.
- Your thanks and hope to hear from them soon.

Now sit back and pride yourself on a job well done.

Putting Your Business On The Internet

Just about anyone can put a web site up on the internet and now days it is quite easy. You have two choices as how to set up your website:

- As a shop window for your company, with contact details etc.
- As a fully working site with ecommerce facilities.

Which ever option you choose, you first need a god domain name. Go to a good domain provider like enom, godaddy, namecheap and spend under £10 on a domain. Choose a domain name that has the word scrapbook in it. This will help with your search engine positioning as well as act as a memory jog to your potential customers.

As A Shop Window

Hop over to hostgator or similar and then buy a monthly hosting account. With that will come a site maker - where you can easily set up a web site using one of thousands of templates. You can add payment processor linkages, forums etc.

The only problem you will have is you want to sell promote or talk about illegal activities, terrorist activities or sex! Also if you want a high usage activity such as MySpace etc.

As A Full Site

You will probably need to get this especially written and designed for you. Put your project on sites like guru/elance/scriptlance etc and find a competitive quote.

Get yourself a PayPal account or similar so that you can take payment on your web site. This is much more secure and quicker than taking checks.

Factors To Remember

Always consider your target market when designing your web site. Include some helpful information about your subject matter but nothing that will give away what you are trying to sell! Ensure that your contact details can be freely found and that details of your company and services are clearly set out.

As you will be asking for money before you deliver something – make your potential customer feel comfortable making payment and tell them what will happen next.

Respond to all enquiries and purchases very quickly. If this is difficult then set up an autoresponder to confirm you have received their enquiry/payment and will get back to them within a few hours. Place references that you have received from past

An Internet Marketing Strategy

Ok, you have got your web site set up, you are sure that it is search engine friendly and you are pretty certain what your customers want. You have identified at least 3 products that you want to promote and you think that they meet your potential customer's needs. So now what?

Well unfortunately the days, that I can remember, of "build it and they will come" have long gone. Unless you promote your web site – no one will know that you are there and no visitors means no sales. So where so you go from here?

Well take a deep breath, a pen and paper and let's start on your Marketing Strategy. Briefly for a new business, with a relatively inexperienced marketer, your strategy will probably include the following options:
- Pay Per Click Advertising
- Article Marketing
- Email Marketing
- Community Marketing
- Classified Advertising

Let's get started – and before you start panicking, you are just writing your Marketing Strategy. This course will explain how to do all of the following.

Profitable New Scrapbooking Business

Your Advertising Kit

For each of your programmes/products

1. Write a short advert – say 50 words.
2. Write a very short advert – say 15 words
3. Write a short article – say about 400 – 600 words.
4. Decide on your keywords – say about 30– 50 words.

Your Marketing Kit

For your web site theme

1. Write at least 6 short auto responder messages.
2. Find or write at least 2 giveaway products.

Your Marketing Tools

1. Your web site
2. An autoresponder
3. A good email account

Put all of these together into your first Marketing Strategy.

1. **Submit your web site to all the major search engines.** This will start to get your web site noticed. As this takes a long time, it needs to be the first thing that you do. You can do this yourself or pay someone else to do this for you.
2. **Set up your autoresponder form** on your web site and load your messages into the autoresponder. Ensure that you offer one of the giveaway products as a bonus for signing onto your ezine. The second giveaway can be set up for message 3 or 4. Your messages should be sent in the following intervals. Day 1,3,7,7,7,7

3. **Set up your download pages**, for your bonus products as well as the products you are selling. Ensure that you provide an extra offer on each download page.
4. **Submit your article** – including your resource box, to about 6 major ezine article sites. Limit yourself to 6 at the moment. Each of these submissions, if accepted will give you a link to your web site. If too many links to your new web site appear very quickly, search engines assume that you have been using "black hat" SEO tactics (a total no no) and will not list your site.
5. **Identify 4 forums** that discuss the topics of your web site. Set yourself up an account name that describes you well. We use the name "Biz Guru" which is our trade mark and name. Set up your signature to include your web site address. You now have 4 good links to your web site.
6. **Answer Questions:** Start answering questions asked within the forums. Do NOT post adverts for your web site or products. Use this time to establish your credentials. If you answer questions well and contribute to the forums, your web site tag will be noticed.

7. **Set up a PPC campaign** – you can start with the smaller search engines first. Take your very small advert and your keywords and use them in your campaign. Most search engines will help you with your choice of keywords. Remember to set a budget and test, test and test again until you get quality and converting traffic.

8. **Set up some classified ads**. You can do this one of two ways: i) choose one or two major sites/email lists and advertise with them. ii) use an ezine ad blaster to send your ad out to numerous low quality places.

9. **Test, Update and Modify**. Review, change and add to your PPC keywords. Submit more articles and adverts. Start tactfully promoting your products in the forums.

Your challenge will be to be listed in the major search engines and then get traffic. Now market your web site like mad. It will take several months to make an impact in the major search engines. So build up your local custom whilst you are doing this. www.GetIntoGoogleFast.com – Does exactly what is says in the domain!

Staff

Expansion means growth, involving people working for you, more jobs to sell, and greater profits. Do not let it frighten you, for you have gained experience by starting gradually. After all - your aim in starting a business of your own was to make money, wasn't it? And expanding means more helpers so you do not have to work your self so hard!

So, just as soon as you possibly can, recruit and hire other people to do the work for you. The first people you hire should be people to handle customer sales.

You can obtain good staff by word of mouth, advertising in your local Job Centre, supermarket etc. Look in your local university and local school and ask amongst friends. You will find a lot of people who want to work part time here - as well as those that are able to work early in the morning or in the evening if you need them.

You can start these people at minimum wage or a bit above, and train them to complete every job assignment in a set timeframe. You might consider hiring people on a contract basis so that if they do not work you do not pay. You do not get loyalty here though.

You should also outfit them in a kind of uniform with your company name on their shirts and jackets. You can find many companies on the internet that will provide these very cheaply.

Customer Contracts

When you are dealing with customers, sometimes things can go wrong. It might be your fault, it might be their fault or it might be no-one's fault -- but if you didn't make a contract, then you will all suffer.

Why Do I Need Contracts?

A contract gives you a sound legal base for your business, and some guarantee that you are going to get paid for your work without you having to ask the customer for payment in advance. In the event of a dispute, the contract lays down what the agreement was so that you can point to it and say what was agreed. If you ever end up having to go to court (let's hope you will not), the contract is what the judge's decision will be based on.

Without a contract, you leave yourself vulnerable and open to exploitation. Someone could claim that the terms they agreed with you were different to what you say they were or that they never signed up for anything at all and so they will not pay.

It is especially common to see big businesses mistreat small ones, thinking that they will not have the knowledge or the money to do anything about it. Essentially, contracts take away your customers' ability to hold non-payment over your head, and give you the ability to hold it over theirs instead.

Profitable New Scrapbooking Business

Written and Verbal Contracts

It is important to point out the distinction in the law between a verbal (spoken) contract and a proper, written one. A verbal contract is binding in theory, but in practice can be very hard to prove. A written contract, on the other hand, is rock-solid proof of what you are saying.

You might think that you are never going to get into a dispute with your customers, but it is all too common to find yourself in a little disagreement.

They will often want to get you to do some 'small' amount of extra work to finish the job or make it better; not realising that doing so would completely obliterate your profit margin.

For this reason, you should be very wary of doing anything with nothing but a verbal contract. On the other hand, if you were incautious or too trusting and only got a verbal contract, it could still go some way towards helping you, especially if there were witnesses.

Will It Be Expensive?

Written contracts do not necessarily need to be formal contracts, which are drawn up by a lawyer with 'contract' written at the top and signed by both parties.

These kinds of contracts are the most effective, but can be expensive to have produced, not to mention intimidating to customers.

The most common kind of written contract, oddly enough, is a simple letter. If you send a customer a letter laying out your agreement before you start work, and they write back to agree to it, that is enough to qualify as a written contract, with most of the protections it affords. It is best to get confirmation from your customer that they have received this contract.

If you are doing high-value work for some clients, though, it could be worth the time and trouble of having your lawyer write a formal contract, or at least of doing it yourself and getting a lawyer to look it over.

Formal contracts will give you more protection if the worst happens, and there is nothing to stop you from making it a one-off expense only by re-using the same contract for multiple customers. **PLEASE: TAKE PROFESSIOANAL ADVICE.**

Contracts for Small Purchases.

Obviously it would be silly to expect everyone who buys some £10 product or service from you to sign a contract, or write back indicating their agreement to your terms. In this situation, you should have a statement of the 'terms and conditions' that your customer is agreeing to by buying from you, and they should have to tick some kind of box indicating their agreement before you send anything.

The Top 5 First Year Mistakes

Even once you have got past the starting-up stage, there are still plenty mistakes to be made, and most of them are going to be made in your make-or-break year -- the first one. Here are the top five things to avoid.

Waiting for Customers to Come to You

Too many people wait for their customers to phone, or come to the door, or whatever. They get one or two customers through luck, but nothing like enough to even begin paying their costs. These people sit around, looking at their competitors doing lots of business, and wonder what they are doing wrong.

You can't be like this. You have to go out there and actively try to find customers. Talk to people, call them, meet with them -- whatever you do, do not just sit there!

Spending Too Much on Advertising

So everyone tells you that the only way to get ahead in business is to advertise. Well, that is true, but you need to make sure that you stick to inexpensive advertising methods when you are starting out. Spending hundreds of dollars for an ad in the local newspaper might turn out to get you very few new customers, and you will have spent your entire advertising budget on it.

Make your money go further with leaflets, direct mail or email -- these are easily targetable campaign methods with high response rates and low costs. Remember that it is always better to spend money on an offer than on an ad, and always better to spend money on an ad than on a delivery method.

Being Too Nice

When you are running your own business, it can be tempting to be everyone's friend, giving discounts at the drop of a hat and making sure that you do not hassle or inconvenience anyone.

That is all well and good, until you find that your Good Samaritan act has just halved your profit margin without lowering the cost to the customer by very much at all.

Sometimes, you need to realise that you have got to be harsh to make a profit. Give people discounts to encourage them to buy or to come back, not because you like them or feel sorry for them. Do not be afraid to be ruthless in your pursuit of business success. Nice guys do not finish last, but they are running in a different race -- one with much less prize money. If that does not bother you, of course, then feel free to go for it.

Not Using the Phone

You'd be surprised just how common phone fears are -- if you are scared of the phone, you are not alone by any means. Many people are terrified of making phone calls, and avoid them wherever possible. I have seen more than one business owner reduced to tears on the phone and trying desperately to hide it from the customer.

You need to try your best to overcome your fears, as talking to customers on the phone is almost as good as meeting them for real. Letters and emails are useless by comparison. The best way to overcome phone fears varies from person to person, but it can often be as simple as making the phone fun, by calling friends and relatives often for a while and getting used to it. Alternatively, try working in telemarketing for a while -- if that does not make normal phone use look like a walk in the park by comparison, then nothing will.

Hiring Professionals for Everything

It can be tempting to think that, since you are starting out, you should just find a company or person to do every little thing you need. Do not hire anyone until the cost of what they do directly benefits your company.

People seem to especially overspend on design services. Will fancy graphics all over your website increase sales? Likewise, a slick brochure often fails to say anything more than 'I'm going to charge you a premium to pay for my expensive brochures'.

Problems You May Have

As in any business you will get problems, sometimes just knowing what you may face is a great help:

- Some customers use office email to correspond with you. Make sure that you are discrete with the headings used on the emails to them.
- Some customers are never satisfied. Just make any reasonable changes that are requested. Similarly some have a very high opinion of their very basic experience. Be polite and patient.
- Some customers may have problems explaining what they want – this is where your product list comes in handy. Make sure that you write down everything that they request and get this agreed to.
- Some customers are very slow in replying – ensure that you give them a time limit to reply and then send two further reminders – telling them when the last one is.
- Some people are not really potential customers so learn to spot those people that will take a lot of your time, "just looking".
- Some people will try to knock your price down, just because they feel they can. Spot those that you can help by lowering your prices a little and steer clear of those that just want a lot for not very much money. You are in business and deserve to make a profit for your efforts.

Time for a Holiday: But How?

When you have been working long and hard at your business for a while, you might feel like you have earned yourself a little break. There are business owners out there who have not taken a real holiday since they started their business -- including some who started their business as long as five years ago!

After all, how can you ever just desert your business and your customers and go bronze yourself on the beach? How can you avoid being on call 24/7 throughout your holiday? Well, everyone deserves some time to themselves at least once a year, if they want to keep being productive and avoid stress. Here's what to do.

Tell People When You Are Going Away.

You can't just disappear when you are running a business -- you need to let people know long in advance that you are not going to be available, and make sure that they have everything they need to manage without you while you are away. It is best to schedule your holiday not to interfere too much with the business.

However much you might want to have your holiday in the summer, it is important to remember that every business has its quiet months, and you should schedule your holiday in the period where they seem to be.

Change Your Voicemail Message.

A quick and simple way to let people know that you have gone away is to change your voicemail message. This allows you to still hear what people have to say when you get back, and stops them from wondering why you never seem to answer your phone.

A good format for the message is as follows: 'Hi, this is [your name] at [company name]. I'm sorry I'm not in the office right now, but I will be back on [give a date]. If you leave a message, I will be sure to get back to you'.

If you work from home do not give a coming back date unless you want to invite the local thief into your home!

Set Up an Email Auto responder.

Similar to a voicemail message, but less commonly used, is the email auto responder. Again, you do not want people to wonder why their emails are going unanswered, so your best bet is to set up your email programme to automatically reply to any email you get with a message saying that you have gone away and will be back very soon.

Example: 'Hello, and thank you for your email. This is an auto responder, as I'm away on holiday until [date]. I have received your email, however, and will respond to it upon my return. I apologies for any inconvenience to you, and I am willing to make an offer of 10% off your next order to make it up to you.'

The special offer for people who get the auto responder is a nice touch -- it makes them feel lucky that they emailed you while you were away, instead of frustrated.

Do not Stay Away Too Long.

Of course, when you go on holiday, you are relying on people being willing to wait for you. That means you can't really take the kids to Disney World for two weeks, or spend a month staying with a friend abroad -- it is just too long to be away from your business for.

You should regard a weekend away as ideal (it avoids the whole problem for the most part), and a week as the maximum you can allow yourself. Do not let people make you feel bad about only taking one-week holidays: after all, you could always have more than one each year.

Get Someone to Look after the Business.

If you really want to get away for longer, or it is essential that your customers do not have any break in service, then you could consider getting someone to look after your business.

This could be an existing member of staff that you make your 'deputy', to be in charge while you are away, or it could be someone who's related to you and has some experience running a business. Enjoy your holiday!

In Conclusion

One of the most important aspects of this business is asking for, and allowing your customers to refer other prospects to you. All of this happens, of course, as a result of your giving fast, dependable service. You might even set up a promotional notice on the back of your business card (to be left at each job is completed) offering money off their next scrapbook service/seminar if they refer you to a new prospect.

This is definitely a high profit business, requiring only an investment of time and organisation on your part to get started. With a low investment, little or no overhead requirement, this is an ideal business opportunity with a growth curve that accelerates at an unprecedented rate.

Brought to You By The Biz Guru
"If you need help with your business – click or brick – we're here to help"
www.StartMyNewBusiness.com

Index:

advertising, 61, 72, 109
Banking, 66, 161
brand, 61, 72, 110, 117, 118
Branding, 110, 117
business card, 182
Business Name, 65, 117
Business Plan, 62, 66
capital, 109
contract, 157, 158, 172, 173, 174
Customer Administration, 162
distributor, 61, 71, 72
Employment Laws, 66
Estimating, 156
hosts, 73
information pack, 158
Insurance, 66
Internet, 165
Invoices, 117
lease, 71
Licenses, 66
loans, 73
marketing, 64, 66, 72, 75, 76, 108

Marketing Material, 118
Order Forms, 117
Packaging, 117, 118
Patents and Trademarks, 65
Permits, 66
postcards, 122
price points, 109
Pricing, 61
Sales, 50
Staff, 64, 72, 161, 171
Staff costs, 72
Stock, 73
Target Audience, 47
Taxes, 66
The Biz Guru, 182
Uniform, 50
Uniforms, 72
upgrades, 109
web site, 64, 65, 117, 118, 165, 166, 170
Your Brochure, 49
Your Business Entity, 65

www.ingramcontent.com/pod-product-compliance
Lightning Source LLC
Chambersburg PA
CBHW022010160426
43197CB00007B/366